THOUGHTS WHILE FLYING HIGH!

Like to Be A Brit For a Few Days?

SIR RICHARD N. DAVIS

Copyright © 2012. Sir Richard N. Davis
All rights reserved.

ISBN: 1475220537
ISBN-13: 9781475220537

This book is dedicated to my dear friend and colleague who helped make this possible years ago and sadly lost his long battle with an incurable blood disease some years ago.

DAVID DOUGHERTY

Sincere thanks and appreciation are extended to:

Elizabeth and Ron Mapp
Kim Fox

For their sterling suggestions, patient proofreading, and endless English ideas.

Table of Contents

Introduction	xi
Real Vignettes about Britain and Brits	1
Acting Greats	2
All Creatures Great and Small	2
Astonishing Statues	3
Bath Cathedral Epitaphs	4
Beds: Four-Poster	4
Beehive Inn (Edinburgh)	5
Bishops and Other Effigies in Cathedrals	6
The Black Prince	6
The Blue Plaques	7
Bone House (St. Leonard's Church, Kent)	9
Broadway B&B (northern Cotswolds)	10
Burghley House (Near Stamford)	11
Buxton Opera House	12
Canal Boat Trips in North London	13
Castle Howard	13
Carlisle Cathedral	15
Ceilidhs and Mauds	16
Chatsworth House	16
Chelsea Pensioners	18
Crooked Spire Church	18
The Crown Jewels	19

(Some) Curiosities of English History	21
Daffodils and Wordsworth and York	22
Day of Remembrance	23
Dean Close School (Cheltenham)	24
Eastnor Castle	25
Edinburgh Princes Street: March in Joy	26
Edinburgh Military Tattoo (Edinburgh Festival)	27
English Form of Government	27
Enigma Code Heroes	30
Eros or Angel?	31
Executioner's Place and the Royal Mile	31
Fairytale Castle	32
Falkirk Wheel and Antonine Wall	33
Farthings: 1279–1960	34
Ferry: Harwich (UK) to Den Hoek (Netherlands)	34
Flint Mines	36
The Flying Scotsman	36
Follies	38
Foreign Medicine and Doctors	39
Fountains Abbey Tunnel	39
The Giant of Cerne	40
Gilbert and Sullivan for One Full Week	41
Glyndebourne—Festival of Opera That's Grand	42
Grampians and Trossachs and Ben Nevis	43
Grizedale Forest and Lake District National Park	44
Guardians of the Queen	44
Guy Fawkes Day	46
Hailes Abbey	46
Half-hangit Maggie	47
Harris Tweeds May Be in Trouble	48
Hat, Wig, Powder, and Other Taxes	48
Hire Cars (Rentals)	50
Holkham Hall	51
Honi Soit Qui Mal Y Pense and The Most Noble Order of the Garter	53
King Alfred the Great	55
King George III and Eton Birthday Boat Procession	57

King George V and the British Empire	58
Lancelot the Gardener	59
Longleat and the Safari	60
Long Man of Wilmington and Others	61
Mayflower	61
Mazes	62
Mermaid Street (Rye, Sussex)	62
Metropolitan Cathedral of Christ the King (Liverpool)	63
Murals and a Statue at Blenheim Palace	63
Musicians of Note (British)	65
National Memorial to the Few	65
The National Trust	66
Number 10 Downing Street	67
Olde Customs and Traditions	67
Boxing Day: 26 December	xx
Oliver Cromwell's Last Hurrah	73
Opera in Edinburgh	74
(A Few) Painters (British): 1700–Present	75
Peas on a Knife	76
Prime Ministers of Note	76
The Proms	77
Pulteney Bridge (Bath)	79
The Queen Mother	79
Rapeseed Oil (UK)	80
Ravens at the Tower of London	81
Rhododendrons and Redwoods	81
Robert de Bruce (1274–1329)	82
Royal Ascot	83
Royal Tidbits	85
St. Bartholomew the Great (Smithfield)	86
St. Mary's Student and His Red MG	87
Savile Row Tailors	88
Seaton's Miniature Tram	88
Shute Barton Manor Home (Devon)	89
Songs in a Town Hall	89

Sports (British):	
Cricket, the Gentleman's Game	91
Rugby	91
Soccer	93
Stained Glass Angels in the High Octagon of Ely Cathedral	94
Standing Stones in Britain	94
Stone of Scone	95
Styling Examples in History	97
Teahouse (Coffeehouse) in Edinburgh	97
Teatime for Brits (and Others)	98
Theme Parks	98
Thetford Salutes Captain Mainwaring (*Dad's Army*)	99
Trains to Bath	100
Trompe L'oeil in England	100
Trooping the Colours	101
Walkways and Canals	102
Warwick Castle (the Castle of Kings) and Kenilworth	103
Whitby Abbey, "The Steps," Abbess Hilda, Bede, and Captain Cook	104
William (UK) and Willem-Alexander (Netherlands)	105
William Rufus, "The Red"	105
Winchester: Capitol, Cathedral, Committed Diver	109
Wootton Bassett's Silent Tribute	110
Writers (British)	111
York	112
Yorkshire Lavender	113
Abbeys and Priories	115
Castles	116
Cathedrals	117
Flower Shows	118
Gardens	119
Great British Heritage Pass	xxx
Manor Homes	119
Museums (London)	120
National Railway Museum	121
Newspapers (London)	140

Parks (London)	122
Performing Arts:	123
Ballet	124
Festivals	124
Music	125
Opera	125
Venues for Ballet, Jazz, Opera, Pop, Rock, Theater	125
Theatres (London)	126
Public Schools	129
Pubs (Publick Houses) in London	127
Pubs (UK)	129
Royal Residences and Palaces	130
Stately Homes	130
Specialty Stores, Fine Shops, Markets (London)	134
Supermarkets	135
Tea Shops (London)	136
Tearooms (UK)	135
Theme Parks and Open-Air Museum	138
Villages of England	133
Northern Counties	133
Midland Counties	133
Eastern Counties	133
Southern Counties	133
Western Counties	134
Traditional English Foods (a Sampling)	131
Transportation	139
Universities and Schools of Higher Learning	132
THESAURUS OF ENGLISH TO AMERICAN WORDS	141
WHERE TO GO FOR SPECIAL HELP	193
Resources and Acknowledgments	196

Introduction

If you plan to fly to Great Britain, then you will want to know as much as possible about that great country before you ever get there. Flying from the United States means a long, overnight trip. Yes, you will be amply fed and given drinks. And you may take naps or even a long sleep. And you will wish to walk and walk to keep your energy levels up and your circulation problems down.

There will probably not be a better chance to read and think about what you will do and where you will be for the next few days? Weeks? Months? Remember, it will be dark outside. You will have your own overhead light. And if you have this book with you on the trip, you can read or reread and use these precious moments before landing to prepare for this exciting trip. This is when *you* will enjoy the most important part of your planning: *Thoughts While Flying High!*

Wouldn't you love to be a Brit for just a few days, maybe more? More than 2.5 million Americans visit the British Isles (United Kingdom) *each year*. You may be one of them! Before you take the step (trip), it would be helpful to learn about what is in that grand country that might help you enjoy being a happier, more informed person.

Just consider this for a moment: some of your heritage has been deeply influenced by the English way of life. The customs, the proper manners, the glorious history, fine art, excellent music, superb architecture, and a host of items relating to the valued traditions of the monarchy. It would take years to learn about all of these incredible elements. The Brits have been a major influence in literature, travel, traditions, customs, and daily living. Their diplomacy and statesmanship is of the highest caliber. We can thank them for standing up to the Axis powers and the Nazis, *twice*. That tiny isle has been a bastion of determination and fierce competitiveness against adversity. Best of all, the English speak good English!

This wee book cannot tell you everything. It may not even be the only way to learn about a fine country and its noble people. But it will give you guidelines of what to expect and how to discover and revel in your newfound insights.

For example, there are sterling lists of abbeys, castles, cathedrals, stately homes, manor houses, government buildings, and royal residences (including addresses). That's just for starters. Did you know that London is considered the gastronomical center of Europe? You are even told about some of the sixty thousand pubs, the many, many restaurants, the fine tea shops all over Britain. You will learn the names of great theatres and places to enjoy fine music, jazz, ballet, and drama. Perhaps even dance!

The transportation is superb: buses, taxis, trains, airlines, and subways (the Tube).

You can find pharmacies (chemists) if you need them. Even well-staffed hospitals and clinics. You are told how and where to get help for anything you suddenly might face.

The most important items in this book that could help you feel rather British will come from almost 3,500 words and phrases used in daily parlance in the UK. And we have enclosed 155 genuine "vignettes" that will help you identify with some real happenings and people that will fill your moments with enjoyment as a would-be Brit.

If this still hasn't tilted your interest across the "pond," then consider one or both great flower shows in Chelsea and Harrogate, plus far more illustrious and well-planned gardens than you can imagine. "A man without a garden is hardly an Englishman!"

There are hundreds of museums and galleries in London alone. And the colleges and universities, among the best in the world, are found in many a shire (county), some of which are among the oldest on the globe. There are theme parks with rides that truly rival the best of American amusement parks.

You will enjoy reading about many diverse traditions and customs and where they are held and when. You will discover untold riches from living in fine hotels or inns. But to best see and reach out to the natives, stay in a B&B, each one of which is monitored and approved by careful inspections. These are real Brits, people who can help you in the smallest and biggest need. They will enrich your trip and your memories.

If you choose to drive (remembering the left side of the road is the "right side"), you will be astonished by all the roads and big motorways that have *no* potholes or breaks in the road!

Believe us, fun travel means good planning. Maybe a tour would be a good start. Or using the trains or buses would fit your needs. There is always a way to get there. Oh yes, and when each day comes to a close, a fine dinner may be just around the corner and a drink or two from a historic and lovely pub may offer a tasty nightcap before retiring to your hotel or inn or B&B for sweet rest. "Flying high gets you there; down-to-earth planning makes it great!" Welcome to one of the most fascinating places in the world!

REAL VIGNETTES
ABOUT BRITAIN AND BRITS

Most people find it rather difficult to relate to other parts of the world, even if they are posted there for some time. Often one finds many events, ideas, and people who make a visit or new home quite attractive, thus helping to establish joy with their "temporary" home.

It is not easy to know enough about any country just by reading or looking at beautiful pictures, although that can be very helpful. One needs to find a way to engage in activities and special moments that help integrate past experience into a new set of circumstances. This can be very taxing and disappointing to some whose expectations are too high. Still others, wanting to be a Brit, for example, believe they can grow through encounters with people and welcome moments that pop up unexpectedly. The following vignettes will *not* always happen to each person—certainly not in the way these stories relate. Just be comforted by the thought that these events *did* happen to real people, giving credence to the possibility of a similar moment happening to any traveler.

Allow these insights to encourage you to be aware of the kindness and sincere courtesy of many people you will meet along your journey. Take a few moments to dust off the newness of the moment and incorporate it into your own wish to learn from each experience and look forward to the next. In simple words: something like one or more of these vignettes *could* happen to you!

Acting Greats

These are just some of the great actors who walked (or still walk) the stages, uttered the magical words, and lent comfort and insight to many a lonely ear. They made a better life seem possible through words and actions. Many faces were seen on the silent screen and ultimately live cinema. These dramatic souls all hail from Britain: Laurence Olivier, Judi Dench, John Gielgud, Maggie Smith, Peter Ustinov, Ian McKellan, Alec Guiness, Helen Mirren, Ralph Richardson, Vivien Leigh, Richard Burton, Joan Plowright, Jack Hawkins, Jessica Tandy, Michael Redgrave, Lynn Redgrave, John Mills, Angela Lansbury, Albert Finney, Edith Evans, Alan Bates, Nigel Hawthorne, Ian Holm, Ben Kingsley, Peter Sellers, Kenneth More, Rex Harrison, Anthony Hopkins, Peter O'Toole, and Claude Rains. There are others who were born in England and spent most of their acting lives in America: Cary Grant, Bob Hope, and Elizabeth Taylor.

All Creatures Great and Small

You don't have to be a Scot to remember James Herriot, his beloved books (eighteen in all), and his uncanny veterinarian sense. He treated rich and poor alike, loving all animals and treating them, often free of charge, whenever and wherever. He was born in Sunderland but spent most of his working life in or near Thirsk and his beloved moors. He and his compatriots ranged far and wide to help those with huge animals and small ones. Most believed in him and loved him, but some of the leaders in Thirsk were jealous of his notoriety and sought to bring most of the fame to Thirsk. He didn't bother with such triviality. It was his death that brought these few to their senses. They are now very proud to call Thirsk his home (he actually lived on a farm in Thirkleby, a crossroads at the time, and not far from Thirsk).

The movie of the same name starred Anthony Hopkins, but it was the ninety episode stories (*All Creatures Great and Small*) of his many dealings with animals and their owners over almost sixty years that was depicted in these telling tales for more than twelve years. They are still available on DVD. The name came from the first verse of the hymn "All Things Bright and Beautiful," in which the above title follows the opening words. James was a devout God-fearing man.

He was honored in later years, and his name became almost household in nature because most people with the love of a good English/Scottish series, and who had any love for all types of animals, knew he was the quintessential veterinary. To honor him the Sunderland football (soccer) team made him an honorary owner and gave him and his dear wife lifetime passes to the games. They rarely missed a game. He died from cancer in 1995 at seventy-eight years of age..

Astonishing Statues

In the heart of Piccadilly Circus there is a huge fountain in the circus (circle) depicting Eros with his whimsical bow and arrow. It was the first time that London was treated to a nude statue of a female on a major street. The fountain was given by Lord Shaftesbury, a noted political giant, and the arrow seems to be pointed down the street, perhaps to open a new way for Brits. Or it may have been intended, as Brits love to twit, at the rear end of a horse with some noble person astride. Who was that man? An adversary? A man of love? No easy answers.

Go just south of this crowded center and you are in Trafalgar Square, so named because it was also the name for Admiral Lord Nelson's greatest victory. There is a majestic structure, Nelson's Column, that is 151 feet tall, supporting an 18-foot statue of Lord Admiral Horatio Nelson, with his right hand over his heart and his left hand at the hilt of his sword, which is touching the ground. The column is constructed of Foggintor granite. The statue faces towards the south, looking distantly to the Admiralty and Portsmouth where Nelson's flagship, HMS *Victory is* still docked. The mall is on his right flank.

The top of the column, at the base of the statue, has bronze acanthus leaves made from the cannon from Nelson's ships. The bottom of the pedestal is made of bronze panels cast from some of the many guns he captured during his four great victories. There are four large and gorgeous bronze lions, taken from the cannon of that last French fleet so decisively beaten by Nelson.

One can see the National Gallery, St. Martin-in-the-Fields church, and the square adjoining the mall through the magnificent Admiralty Arch. Look south to Whitehall, east to the Strand and South Africa House, north to Charing Cross Road (considered the center of old London Town), and west to Canada House.

To underline the significance of these offerings to the gallant memory of a great British hero, Trafalgar Square ranks as the fourth most popular tourist attraction on earth with more than fifteen million visitors per year.

Bath Cathedral Epitaphs

Most every church, abbey, and cathedral has a cemetery or chapel or someplace where they honour the dead who were members of that churchly center at one time. Many of them have old, old gravestones that tell real stories about real people, even though most of it is in short form, like a *Reader's Digest*. But there is one cathedral in Bath that takes time to honour their notables both in the massive stone floors and in the walls. Curiously, they also poke fun at some who were less than admirable. There are poems, limericks, and flat-out humorous "tributes" to some long-ago heroes or villains of that churchly lot. Such discoveries are worth the effort because it gives a flavour of another time and yet has the power to evoke a laugh or wry smile.

Beds: Four-Poster

Many castles, palaces, and stately homes have large and copious bedrooms. The windows are tall and the ceilings are very high, which allows four-poster beds to be the central part of major bedrooms, primarily for heads of each home and also for visiting dignitaries. There is usually a canopy on the top of the large bed and a thick mattress beneath. The bed is often elevated above the floor and may be resting on thick boards that cover the entire underside of the bed. The canopy protects the top of the bed from rats and other vermin that might come from the ceiling or other sources. The curtains may be drawn to prevent animals from invading the bed. It also affords privacy and concealed intimacy.

Beehive Inn (Edinburgh)

Edinburgh has had many fine inns that go way back in history. One such place began as a stop for the carriage trade, most especially the important transportation routes for the Royal Mail stagecoaches. They delivered mail and other items to the various venues in England and Scotland. They were often accosted by highwaymen who forced them to "stand and deliver." Many items were purloined and a few drivers were murdered. Those who survived the treachery of the roads and the challenge of the weather ended up at fine inns such as the Beehive. There they could get a fine meal or enjoy the challenge of devouring a "yard of ale" to prove their strength and endurance, not to mention drinking acumen.

The Beehive was so named because it was conically shaped to appear as a hive; the inside was cleverly covered with stucco-like plaster with rugged and quite rough edges to show its uniqueness. All this was covered in a yellow-orange paint to mimic the inside of a genuine beehive.

While this fine restaurant was once a grand inn and adjoined to the Rafters Restaurant for good food, it is now a partial relic of yesteryear. Above Rafters was a door from the cell for a condemned man that once formed part of the old Tolbooth. The Royal Mail stopped using this key place many years ago. It is a genuine touch of the past and well recognized, even today, by beer connoisseurs and those who love to sit and talk and drink in the beer garden in the back, or be in the "sitooterie," where there are pavement tables in the heart of the north side of the Grassmarket.

Years ago the writer was a student at the School of Divinity of the University of Edinburgh. He and his best friend from the university were nearing the end of term and chose to escort two lovely ladies to the Beehive

Inn. The food and drinks were fabulous. Before departing, the ladies went to the powder room(loo). Both lads discovered that they had left their wallets with checkbooks and cash in their digs. How embarrassing! One lad walked to the maître d' with the problem. The maître d' looked at the university badges on the blazers and decided they were a good risk. He bade them come back the next day, or when it was convenient, to settle the bill. It was done the next morning. How incredible! It shows the enormous trust and warmth of the real Scots. *If* you go, you will discover a winsome and most charming place with copious changes to the interior. The name remains and so do the ghosts who seem to prefer the well-stocked cellars. Oh yes, you do still have to pay the bill!

Bishops and Other Effigies in Cathedrals

Many cathedrals have tombs, some with effigies of bishops, and even their wives, often beside these tombs. There are all kinds of interesting ways to honor noteworthy princes of the church. Some have their mitres and clerical bands cast in stone. Still others have a dog or cat by their side. One even has a lion at his feet. Most have their hands clasped over their chests. Some hold their hands in a prayerful position. But the most incredible one is the bishop lying on his side so he can see, presumably, those who gaze upon him. The sculptor in Ely Cathedral even carved his eyes as if they were open and able to look at those who stopped to gaze. Many have angels or cherubs behind or above and some even beside the crypt. Most are wearing ecclesiastical slippers. The folds in their robes are so realistic one might expect the honorific to rise and bless us.

The Black Prince

Canterbury is known for many things. In the heart of this great city is the walled area that surrounds the cathedral. Many quality items are in the various chapels and in the undercroft. There is a very special area adjacent to the Great Altar and just behind the choir. The Black Prince is shown in full armor, gold-plated, yet cast in a black tunic and appointments.

He died at forty-five years of age, having become the greatest military figure of the medieval years. His most startling victories were over the French in some major battles of the Hundred Years War. His only son became King Richard II. The knight's real name was Edward, Prince of Wales. His father: Edward III.

A tragic counterpoint to this great warrior was the horrific murder of St. Thomas à Becket, archbishop and martyr. He was killed in the same Canterbury Cathedral by ruthless knights many years later. Huge brass words mark the spot where he breathed his last breath.

The Blue Plaques

There are many distinguished people who have lived, worked, or been part of something special in England. Where one of these events occurred there is a blue plaque on the front of the building commemorating the person, date of birth and death, and contribution to England and humanity. Here are a few of the more than eight hundred names:

Henry Brooks Adams	Historian
Matthew Arnold	Poet and critic
J. M. Barrie	Author, creator of *Peter Pan*
Sir Max Beerbohm	Caricaturist, author, and parodist
Anne Bronte	Writer
Rupert Brooke	Poet
Sir Edward Burne-Jones	Artist
Lord Byron (first plaque)	Poet
Howard Carter	Egyptologist, discovered King Tut's tomb
Charlie Chaplin	Actor, moviemaker
Winston Churchill	Prime minister
Joseph Conrad	Polish-born British novelist
Captain James Cook	Circumnavigator and explorer
Charles Darwin	Naturalist

THOUGHTS WHILE FLYING HIGH!

Charles Dickens	Novelist
T. S. Eliot	Poet
Arthur Conan Doyle	Creator of Sherlock Holmes
Dame Edith Evans	Actress
Michael Faraday	Scientist
E. M. Forster	Novelist
Mahatma Gandhi	Indian PM, leader, and guru
Graham Greene	Writer
George Frideric Handel	Composer
Stanley Holloway	Actor and singer
Samuel Johnson	Lexicographer, poet, and critic
John Keats	Poet
John F. Kennedy	Politician, president of the United States
John Maynard Keynes	Economist
Rudyard Kipling	Poet and story writer
Charles Laughton	Actor
T. E. Lawrence	"Lawrence of Arabia"
Joseph Lister	Physician and chemist
John Masefield	Poet laureate
Herman Melville	Author of *Moby-Dick*
A. A. Milne	Author of *Winnie the Pooh*
Samuel F. B. Morse	American painter and inventor of Morse code
Lord Louis Mountbatten	Last Viceroy of India
Wolfgang Amadeus Mozart	Composer
Isaac Newton	Natural philosopher
Anna Pavlova	Prima ballerina
Samuel Pepys	Diarist and Secretary to the Admiralty
Alexander Pope	Poet
Ezra Pound	Poet
Joseph Priestley	Scientist, philosopher, and theologian
Sir William Ramsay	Discover of the Noble Gases
Joshua Reynolds	Painter
Vita Sackville-West	Writer and gardener
Robert Louis Stevenson	Scottish novelist of *Treasure Island*
J. R. R. Tolkien	Writer

William Turner	Artist
Vincent van Gogh	Painter
Sam Wanamaker	Visionary, recreator of Shakespeare's Globe
H. G. Wells	Writer
Oscar Wilde	Wit and dramatist
Virginia Woolf	Novelist and critic
Sir Christopher Wren	Architect
William Butler Yeats	Irish poet and dramatist
Emile Zola	French novelist

This is a humble grouping of some key personalities who were in London for some reason, including living there. For a complete list of the plaques and their locations in London, contact Ask.com encyclopedia or go directly to www.ask.com/wiki/List_of_blue_plaques.

Bone House (St. Leonard's Church, Kent)

What is an *ossuary?* It is a receptacle or vault for bones of the dead. In this case it is a crypt on the lower level of the highest and largest church in Hythe, Kent. In days gone by, Hythe was lively and the middle of five Cinque Ports between Hastings and Romney to the west and Dover and Sandwich to the east. King Edward established the ports in 1155 and allowed each town to keep legal fees from court cases if they, in return, would supply sailors and ships when needed by the Crown. Increased income and plenty to do made these towns very comfortable and wealthy.

Now we have to look at those who may have lived there years ago and who now are part of the crypt of dry bones, more than two thousand of them from every part of the body. These bones are all stacked and marked. Then there is a huge pile of bones, some eight thousand, that have yet to be marked and shelved.

You can see different sizes and shapes and guess the genders on some. And you can see wound cuts, deformities, and other remnants of bad times. There is a table of jawbones with teeth that are in surprisingly good shape. Maybe they had not yet found sugar or tobacco.

Where do they come from? Some opine they are leftovers from some battle or perhaps a plague, such as the Black Death. Maybe they are bones from hospitals or other places where people died without any relatives by their side. Or, worst of all, perhaps they are left over from those reopened graves and vaults that contained bodies that had turned into bones only. I do believe the soul rises to heaven on death; just the body remains and slowly ends in bones. We can guess there are people who are just dying to know the answer to these mysteries!

Broadway B&B (northern Cotswolds)

By chance I came upon a lovely old home at the farthest edge of a most attractive cul-de-sac. It was not distinctive in architecture, but soft in its rather butterscotch colouring and warmly enriched by a pair of wee gardens that truly reflected the love of nature and latent ability of the lady who owned this small cottage. She grew and nurtured many varieties of flowers and shrubs.

The inside of her home was rather simple, highlighted by the tea sets and a period fireplace that would be great in the cold hours. The rooms were filled with dainty memorabilia and quaint relics of another day. And the mistress of the house was both informative and kind. Her directions to fine places to eat and her insights into the art and furniture of Broadway were worth the stay.

The real moment of truth came when retiring for the night. The room was reasonably large and very neatly appointed to make even the most tested visitor anxious to retire beneath the gentle covers, surrounded by soft paintings, with an artifact or two on each side of this bedtime invitation.

But the best was just ahead: getting to the loo for any and all reasons. I climbed a very tall and steep ladder, pulling myself up and into the upper attic of this curious arrangement. The water ran cold for a long minute. The floor was cool, even though it was summer. And the commode was of another age. The tub was one that had "olden times" flowing from its majestic size, yet buttressed by the "modern plumbing" that allowed a full and (finally) warm flow of very welcome waters. The crowning touch: when upright and moving you must keep your head bent or you will crack your "bean" numerous times. Testy? Yes, but a truly vintage moment.

Burghley House

There are those who believe this is one of the most beautiful and well-planned houses one can imagine. And it is in a wonderful small town (Stamford, Lincolnshire) that often attracts moviemakers. The town is hilly and filled with beautiful old homes, very quaint shops, tearooms, and one grand old hotel that was a major stop for stagecoache coming from London or even Lincoln.

This house is one of the "prodigy houses." In the mid-1500s those who built prodigy houses had lots of money, had a great desire to build and show extravagant homes, and they attracted very fine architects and stylists.

Sir William Cecil, a devoted consultant and statesman and dear friend of Queen Elizabeth I, received this gift of a huge estate as gratitude from her majesty. Other prodigy house owners included Sir Christopher Hatton and his outlandish house in Holdenby in Northamptonshire; Sir William More and his rebuilt Loseley House in Surrey; Robert Dudley, Earl of Leicester, the queen's favorite, was also a strong patron of Kenilworth Castle in Warwickshire; along with Sir John Thynne and the magnificent Longleat House in Wiltshire. (You will read something about each place in this book.)

Burghley House took some thirty-two years to build, from 1555 to 1587. It was done almost without Cecil because he was such a busy diplomat, confidant, and court advisor. He later became the High Treasurer in 1572.

His best advisor seemed to be a Henryk who was a master stonemason from Antwerp. He fashioned the east side of the house, then he started laying out the remainder of the house: a long courtyard with a great hall at one end and a grand gatehouse at the other. If you could look at it from on high you would see what looked like a giant *E* in honour of Elizabeth. You can't see that today because the northwest wing was demolished in the eighteenth century.

The exterior remains the same, surfaced with Barnack rag,' a limestone from Northamptonshire, and there are many gorgeous windows—some with stained glass, some in transomed and mullioned windows. The stained glass is most evident in the chapel.

As you approach the house from the drive, after passing the opening to the stables and garages and the lustrous shop, you can see the many trees and bright plots of flowers and a winding drive to the front entrance. If you look up, which you will wish to do, there are many cupolas, chimneys, and obelisks, and even some that look a tiny bit like the tops of minarets. The roof is so complex and filled with endless projections that you will relate to Daniel Defoe when he said this roof made the house look "more like a town than a house...the towers and pinnacles, so high and placed at such a great distance from one another, look like so many distant parish churches in a town and a large spire covered with lead, over the clock in the centre, looks like the Cathedral or chief Church of that town."

Inside it is even more majestic with the many, many rooms, each filled with something special and artistic. There are important rooms in the baroque style, complete with exquisite plaster ceilings and delicately carved woodwork and paneling. The most gorgeous touch of all starts with the awesome ceiling and wall paintings by Verrio, the great Italian master. You dare not miss the George Rooms. And you will be overwhelmed by the total look and feel in the Heaven Room.

The art is endless and priceless: you will find artwork by Pieter Brueghel, Rembrandt, Thomas Gainsborough, Joos an Cleve, Sir Geoffrey Kneller, and others.

You must also look carefully at the marvelous work on the wrought iron gates, especially by the gatehouse. And don't miss the enormous kitchen. Never last are the landscaping miracles of "Capability" Brown.

Buxton Opera House

If you choose to go to Buxton and its lovely environs, you will find The Square and the 902-seat opera house, which was built in 1903 to a design by the great theatre architect Frank Matcham, who also created the London

Palladium and the London Coliseum. You will also be delighted to be in Derbyshire, which has many exciting and wonderful places of culture and gardening.

The opera house was not planned exclusively as an opera house, but as a theatre, which ran until 1927. Then came the "talkies," which lasted until 1932, when movies began in earnest and the opera house became a cinema. It turned to summer theatre festivals from 1936 to 1942, some indebted to the Old Vic Company. It then returned to being a cinema, closing in disrepair in 1976 and then renovated in 1979.

From that time forward it has been open for stage productions and some 450 works in comedy, children's shows, drama, concerts, pantomime, dance, and opera. There is a full-time technical staff and town volunteers for house duties such as bartending and ushering.

Canal Boat Trips in North London

The Regent's Canal has been around for more than 180 years. It goes from Camden Lock to the London Zoo and other venues. One can even walk along the towpath to the historic, and still *very* active, rail station: King's Cross. The walk takes forty minutes and is filled with flora and fauna and marvelous old, and a few new, homes, and lots of pubs and inns and other historic spots. It is worth the trip. And you can reach the docks by the Tube or coaches. There are more than 2,500 miles of navigable canals in England and many, many narrow boats for hire: for traveling, for eating, for sleeping, and to visit pubs and inns.

Castle Howard

The majesty and allure of this awesome castle is not the battlements or the stone walls, or the long and gorgeous roads leading up and into this massive estate. It starts very simply with brilliant architecture and thousands of acres of woodland forest and well-tended gardens. It has been called "Yorkshire's Eden." The landscape is dotted with unusual and provocative buildings that lure one inside to discover a mysterious unknown.

This glorious landscape, filled with rustling leaves on tall trees and a thousand-plus acres of gardens and sweetgrass, is bordered on one side by a gorgeous lake and on the other by a façade of seeming fortress and gates. This is the idyllic and memorable home of the Howards. The castle was begun in 1699 and took nearly one hundred years to complete, and the family still adds to it and restore superb furnishings and art. The castle is also noted for its huge dome, which is the largest and first of its kind in England. Sadly, it suffered a severe fire a number of years ago. Gratefully, it was carefully restored, along with the magnificent staircase that winds up ever so high.

The key to the castle's successful collections and quintessential growth has been the devotion to sheer elegance and extraordinary artistry. It is there in abundance.

Start with the great art of Canaletto, then Panini and even Zuccarelli. Then came Marieschi and Bellotto. These were the Italian compadres.

Then there arose a glad time with Joshua Reynolds, Johan Zoffany, William Marlow, and the great Thomas Gainsborough.

If you think you have had enough (or how can anyone have so much?), then think again. Then came Bassano, Bedoli, Carracci, Domenichino, Gentileschi, and the inimitable Titian.

Catch your breath and gaze upon the works of William Morris, Edward Burne-Jones, and Walter Crane, some with great decorative skills; others who could paint murals and even ceilings.

Then they invited the Pre-Raphaelites and English artists including Lord Leighton, G. F. Watts, and others from the Etruscan school of painters.

If these do not satisfy your cultured menu, then look at the broad array of exquisite porcelain from Chelsea, Meissen, Derby, and Sevres. There are flower painters and the awesome Chinese porcelain that looks like a huge pagoda with tiny openings for either candles or small flowers.

There are antique busts, small and large statues, marble columns, and tabletops. There is even a stone corridor, undecorated but inviting. It helps unveil the vivid and imaginative architecture and sculptural allure of the Great Hall.

One cannot miss the Kelly murals or the William Morris screen (three finely embroidered panels from a set of eight depicting figures of women, based loosely around Chaucer's poem "The Legend of Good Women."

And then you must see the wine cooler. It's enormous! It was presented to Lord Morpeth (later Seventh Earl of Carlisle) following his defeat in the election to parliament of 1841. What a grand "consolation prize." It was made in Leeds (just west of York) for more than a thousand guineas (worth more than three hundred thousand dollars today). Basically it was made of native bog oak, stained black, and French polished and mounted in silver gilt. The Lord's coat of arms adorns each side, and close by are the twenty-five polling places of the district of West Riding. The lid is surmounted by the Howard lion crest and the scroll.

You need to discover the immense world, carried on the back of Atlas and surrounded y a sweet pool of water and looking out and down the magnificent terraces that lead almost to Malton to the south.

Before leaving, take an aroma-filled walk in the beauteous rose garden.

Carlisle Cathedral

This was a priory, founded in 1122, and located in the upper northwest area of England, almost to the Scottish border. The diocese was established in 1132 and then came vast changes to the cathedral. Most of the original buildings are gone, but one key element remains: the great east window. Of note are the choir stalls, previously occupied by the monks. They installed hand-carved misericords, and some think that this combination helped keep the men awake.

Of vast importance is the incredible blue ceiling in the nave with its sparkling stars. Add in the upper windows, from the fourteenth century, the lower lights replacing older windows, and the other windows depicting events in the life of Christ. All of these features help make a very impressive and worship-centered edifice. Experience the stone carvings on the capitals around the choir and the sculpture of the *Blessed Virgin and Child* by Vasconcellos. At the upper edge of Derbyshire you come in contact with very fine architecture, incredible remnants of history, and superb art.

Ceilidhs and Mauds

Scots are their own beings. They have traditions that lead into many multifaceted activities for each clan, most of which come to the forefront several times a year. *Ceilidhs* are regular gatherings of each clan. *Mauds* are large gatherings of *all* the clans, highlighted by competitions in sports, music, even literature and lesser activities, inspired mainly by games played for centuries.

Though not a Scot, I was invited to a ceilidh (Clan McKay) and became a regular (honorary) member who sang and danced at each one. It was great! When it came time for the annual maud (music, in summer), they needed someone to sing. They chose me. The honor was great. Sadly, I had to return to the States the same month they wanted my voice. If you have Scottish heritage or know a good, solid Scot, then do see if you can be invited to a clan ceilidh. You will never forget it.

Chatsworth House

There are a few genuine treasure houses in England. Chatsworth is truly one of them. It is owned by one family. It is in the Peak District of Derbyshire, an elegant setting from any approach. The land was purchased in 1549 for six hundred pounds, and construction began in 1552 by Sir William Cavendish. He did not live to see it in its final form. His widow, Bess of Hardwick, completed the construction and bequeathed the house to her son Henry, who later sold it to his brother William. He became the First Earl of Devonshire in 1618. The house was later rebuilt by the Fourth Earl/First Duke from 1685 to 1707.

Only twenty-six rooms are available for public viewing; the other one hundred rooms are private and for the family. One can see the library, which was a conversion from the First Duke's Long Gallery and refitted by the Sixth Duke; the marvelous Painted Hall, the First Duke's original ceremonial entrance hall; and the Great Dining Room, where the first meal was served for the princess who later became Queen Victoria in 1832. You will be reverently amazed when you enter the gorgeous chapel built by the First Duke, and it has remained as built ever since.

The collection of art, including sculpture and special ceilings by Laguerre, comes from the intense and imaginative designs from the many generations of owners. One must appreciate Thomas Archer, the architect, and Sir Jeffry Wyattville, who later designed the arch leading to the entrance. The Entrance Hall, formerly the kitchen, was the work of James Paine.

Here are some of the many artistic items and touches that give great glory to this massive house: a Greek bust of Alexander the Great, a Roman portrait bust of Emperor Antoninus Pius from the first century, and Sir Francis Chantrey's bust of King George IV.

The paintings seem endless. In the entrance you will see paintings by Sir Edwin Landseer, Carlo Maratti, and Gaspard Dughet. Then you will gaze on the beautiful portraits painted by Sir Peter Lely and Jan Baptist Weenix.

Corridors are filled with artistry, including paintings by French, Flemish, and Italian artists: Wouwermans, van Lint, Francken the Younger, Verdoel, Courtois, Poelenburch, Castiglione, Turchi, Mola, Brandi, Solimena, Carracci, and Zuccarelli.

The great artist William Kent designed some mahogany furniture, including fine cabinets and noble beds. See Roman busts from the second and third centuries plus a fine bust of Aphrodite and another bust by Lorenzo Bartolini.

Four hundred and fifty years of grand planning and purchases have enriched the interior most vividly. It also includes wondrous paintings by Rembrandt, Landseer, Gainsborough, and Freud, and sculptures by Canova and Frink.

The thousand-acre park was landscaped by "Capability" Brown and covers many gardens, a man-made lake that feeds water to the cascades, and the giant rockeries. The cascade alone is a marvel to experience and close by is a maze that is both daunting and delightful. You will enjoy the canal and the gravity-fed fountain—capable of emitting a jet of water some ninety metres in the air—and five miles of walks in the big garden, where you will see rare trees, massive shrubs, temples, a cottage, a kitchen and the Rose Gardens.

Children are not forgotten. They can find their way through a maze, paddle in the cascade, see the tallest gravity-fed fountain, find the willow tree that also became a fountain, and see the "giant foot," the trompe l'oeil violin, and the Rolls-Royce jet engine fan. And don't forget the farmyard with chickens, cows, goats, horses, fish, pigs, and sheep. They can get close to the animals and even see a demo of milking every afternoon. Not to be missed are the commando nets, slides, swings, spiral chute, sand, and water play areas.

Last, but of great importance, are the many jewels and embroidery. You will leave feeling you have seen a gem, a treasure house.

Chelsea Pensioners

For many years there have been loyal servants of the Crown who serve most specifically in the Royal Hospital at Chelsea. They are carefully chosen and are faithful in helping with patients, nurses, and other personnel. They are given a virtual lifelong contract, some serving into their 90s. They wear the classic red coats and often add their miniature medals for special days. It is an honour given only to the few. They are supplied with room, board, and garments, plus a modest stipend in addition to their military pension. The heroes of yesteryear are not forgotten.

Crooked Spire Church

The largest church in Derbyshire is St. Mary and All Saints, also known as the "Crooked Spire Church." It was built in the late thirteenth century and was completed in 1360. It is significant because of its tall, tall spire—some 228 feet off the ground. The spire was straight and true when erected. Now it leans almost nine and one-half feet from the center. It is truly twisted today. Why? It had to withstand the thirty-two tons of lead tiles placed on top of that awesome spire. What a "weighty" problem!

The church is still in use and even has daily tours from the ground up. What a curious spire! Where is it? Chesterfield, which is close to Chatsworth House.

The Crown Jewels

"The oldest items in the current coronation regalia, dating from the Restoration, were made for King Charles I. The original ones were destroyed by Oliver Cromwell following the execution of Charles I in 1649, as they were considered to be redundant in an appalling act of historical vandalism. Cromwell had the entire collection sold or melted down and made into coin.

"Look at what is missing: The state crown of Alfred the Great, the most precious crown of St. Edward the Confessor, state crown of King Henry VIII, along with sceptres, swords, burial regalia, and many items stripped from the rich shrine of Edward the Confessor in Westminster Abbey by Henry VIII. The *only* item in the present collection to survive the Commonwealth is the golden ampulla and spoon (used in the coronation ceremony to anoint the monarch's head, palms, and breast with holy oil.)

"The Imperial Crown of State contains many surviving jewels: Edward the Confessor's sapphire, set in the Maltese cross at the top of the crown. It had been part of his ring and was buried with him. The tomb was opened and the ring removed and placed again in a crown worn by Henry I.

"There is a ruby adorning the centre of the Crown of State. It once belonged to the King of Granada, who was murdered by Pedro the Cruel, King of Castille. He presented it to the Black Prince in gratitude for his military assistance at the Battle of Navaretto in 1367. Richard II (Edward's son) inherited it and had it with him when he surrendered to future King Henry IV at Flint, Wales, in 1399. Henry later usurped the throne, Richard was murdered, and Henry V wore this ruby in his crown atop his helmet at the Battle of Agincourt. A bejeweled gold fleuron was struck off this crown and lost in this battle. The ruby was similarly worn by Richard III in his crown at the Battle of Bosworth in 1485. When Richard was killed during the fighting, the ruby and crown famously rolled under a hawthorn bush, were retrieved by Lord Stanley, and were placed on the head of the victorious Henry Tudor.

"This very precious crown also has pearls worn as earrings by Elizabeth I. Within the jewel-encrusted base is the huge diamond called the "Second Star of Africa This was cut from the Cullinan Diamond, the largest diamond ever mined. It was given to Edward VII who had it set in the crown. This truly priceless crown contains: 2,783 diamonds, 17 sapphires, 277 pearls, 11 emeralds, and 5 rubies.

"The new monarch is always crowned with St. Edward's Crown. It is a golden crown encrusted with diamonds, rubies, pearls, emeralds, and sapphires. This one was a replacement for the one sadly destroyed by Cromwell. This crown has been used in the coronation of every monarch since Queen Victoria. She thought it to be too heavy and was crowned with a lighter state crown.

"Also quite impressive is the crown made for Queen Elizabeth (the Queen Mother). This contains the Koh-i-Noor, or Mountain of Light, diamond, Indian in origin. It goes back to the thirteenth century and was presented to Queen Victoria by the East India Company in 1850. A curious legend says any woman wearing this diamond will have good fortune; any man, and there were many, will have a violent end.

"The Imperial Crown of India was made for the visit of King George V to Delhi as Emperor of India. It has six thousand diamonds with rubies, sapphires, and emeralds.

"The George IV State Diadem was made for the coronation of George IV in 1820. It was designed to circle the velvet cap worn by the king on his journey to Westminster Abbey.

"The diadem was worn by Queen Victoria at her coronation, when it was reset with jewels to replace those hired by George IV. It is composed of four diamond pave set cross pattee alternating with four bouquets of rose, shamrock, and thistle. The front cross pattee is set with a four-carat canary-coloured diamond. It was left by Queen Victoria in her will to the crown and is often worn by the reigning queen at the state opening of parliament.

"The largest cut diamond in the world is contained in the Royal Sceptre with the cross. Made of gold and three feet in length, it also contains an enormous amethyst and a superb emerald. There are several other sceptres in this area.

"The Orb, a golden globe topped by a diamond-encrusted cross, dates to 1661 for the coronation of King Charles II and is symbolic of the world ruled by Christianity. It is held in the monarch's left hand during the coronation ceremony. The jeweled cross that surmounts the orb reflects the monarch's title of Defender of the Faith. A smaller orb was made in 1689 for the joint coronation of William III and Mary."

Source: English Monarchs, www.englishmonarchs.co.uk/crown_jewels.htm.

(Some) Curiosities of English History

The Royal Oak Foundation, an American arm of the National Trust of England, finds some wondrous and most interesting tidbits from time to time. To wit: 6.5 feet is the height of the huge dollhouse that resides in Servants' Hall at Wallington near Morpeth. These gorgeous items date back to 1835, including the famous Mouse House. You must look sharply through two keyholes and a mouse hotel.

Imagine that a human skeleton, seven feet in length, was found in 1870 by workmen at Dunster Castle in Somerset. It was found in a tiny cell in which a prisoner had been locked up and apparently forgotten!

If you love to see many and great things at a distance, you need to visit the Iron Age hill fort at Croft Ambrey, near Croft Castle in Herefordshire. Yes, you really can, on a reasonably clear day, see fourteen counties.

It's always been tough to be a soldier. In the times when the Romans were in England, there were many soldiers bivouacked at the Housesteads Fort, on Hadrian's Wall, where there were thirty seats in the latrine. Rather cozy, wouldn't you say?

Nine hundred acres (365 hectares) fill the oak forest that is Horner Wood on the Holnicote Estate in west Somerset. This is the largest woodland are dating back to the Iron Age.

We think we are productive (and are often). What about the Finch Foundry in the nineteenth century? Workers produced four hundred tools a day—without modern technology. Tools included sickles, scythes, and shovels. In the cold, dogs sat on laps to give warmth to the workers.

Most remarkable is the incredible chandelier at Polesden Lacey. It is filled with four thousand pieces of glass, which take two days to dust and a week to clean, one prism at a time.

Thanks to "The List" from *National Trust Magazine,* Autumn 2011

Daffodils and Wordsworth and York

Each spring, often beginning as early as March, and extending into early May, daffodils cover the landscape of York, both the old city and the new. They're on the hills, in the valleys, at the edge of streets and pavements (sidewalks), and even around and on top of the long and glorious walls surrounding the old city. This is a massive and annual event. People estimate the numbers of daffodils to be somewhere between five hundred thousand and five million. Whatever the real numbers, it is truly gorgeous!

Perhaps it was his sister who first talked about it. Perhaps it was because daffodils were among his favorite flowers. Here is what Wordsworth said:

I wandered lonely as a cloud
That floats on high o'er vales and hills,
When all at once I saw a crowd,
A host of golden daffodils;
Beside the lake, beneath the trees,
Fluttering and dancing in the breeze.
For oft, when on my couch I lie
In vacant or in pensive mood,
They flash upon that inward eye
Which is the bliss of solitude;
And then my heart with pleasure fills,
And dances with the daffodils.
William Wordsworth, from "I Wandered Lonely as a Cloud"

SIR RICHARD N. DAVIS

Day of Remembrance

Every country that has been affected by the horrors and enormous casualties inflicted by both the First and Second World Wars have sought to have a Memorial Day, Armistice Day, National Honor Day, or Remembrance Day. The latter is celebrated in the UK. *Every* year since the Crimean War the country has had important acts of contrition and remembrance for each and every soldier, sailor, marine, and flyer who ever fought and died for God and country.

The queen, after the military and governmental leaders have placed their wreaths, puts her large wreath at the front of the great Cenotaph in London, steps back, bows her head briefly, and stands alone to honour those heroes of many conflicts. This is the only time a British monarch bows his or her head for any reason (she did, however, bow her head as Diana's funeral cortege passed).

On each 11 November , at precisely 11 a.m., the entire country stops for two full minutes when "The Last Post" is sounded by a bugle. Yes, this silence includes cars, buses, taxis, pedestrians, those at work, those at home, or those at leisure. They bow their heads and silence prevails. I have been in London and other large venues and experienced this unusual event. It is eerie. It is awesome. And it is *very* moving. One can hardly imagine one of the largest and great cities of the world stopping completely for two *full* minutes. The silence ends when the bugle intones "Reveille," (the "Rouse"), followed by the recitation of "The Ode of Remembrance," more commonly known as the poem "For the Fallen."

Here is the fourth stanza of Laurence Binyon's famous poem:
They shall grow not old, as we that are left grow old;
Age shall not weary them, nor the years condemn.
At the going down of the sun and in the morning,
We will remember them.

Perhaps the most poignant description of these awesome moments was in the *Manchester Guardian* of 12 November 1919:
"The first stroke of eleven produced a magical effect.

"The tram cars glided into stillness, motors ceased to cough and fume, and stopped dead, and the mighty-limbed dray horses hunched back upon their loads and stopped also, seeming to do it of their own volition.

"Someone took off his hat, and with a nervous hesitancy the rest of the men bowed their heads also. Here and there an old soldier could be detected slipping unconsciously into the posture of 'attention.' One elderly woman, not far away, wiped her eyes, and the man beside her looked white and stern. Everyone stood very still…The hush deepened. It had spread over the whole city and became so pronounced as to impress one with a sense of audibility. It was a silence which was almost pain…And the spirit of memory brooded over it all."

If ever you are there, you will *never* forget it, as well as the ones you also honour on the other side of the Atlantic, or wherever your native land exists.

It needs to be mentioned that this day is also known as Poppy Day, a time to buy an artificial poppy from a member of the Royal British Legion, a charity devoted to the support of all war veterans, and to wear it proudly. The poppies reflect Flanders Field and other wartime sites in the poppy fields of the Netherlands.

Dean Close School (Cheltenham)

This very valued school began in 1886 as an evangelical boys' boarding school, named after a rector of Cheltenham, Francis Close. The prime purpose of the school was to educate and instill lifelong principles.

The school grew to more than two hundred students because it was rather inexpensive and sound. Teaching salaries were low, but the quality of education was never compromised.

The school bought the "Big Field" across the road and used the thirteen new acres for sports. It was admitted to the Headmasters' Conference of leading public schools. The school also developed a house system urging upperclassmen to take on new some responsibilities. The Great Depression slowed the growth and cut into new enrollment. During the war the lads were evacuated to their schools, bringing down the numbers until the school almost had to close.

The school expanded after the war and was among the first to allow girls on campus. A theatre was also started along with drama training. The senior school had grown to 485 pupils and the junior school (now prep school) to 250.

The school rescued Tewkesbury Abbey's school and inherited the acclaimed Schola Cantorum as a new choir school, which soon produced the BBC Chorister of the Year. Then came a pre-prep school, which started catering 140 pupils.

Sports to this day are high priority, and the hockey team is very well known and quite successful. A number of students have become known internationally in sports, drama, music, and art, and their performances have won high honors at the sell-out performances of the Edinburgh Fringe.

The school has had strong representation in the armed services, the church, academia, medicine, law, conservation, business, and the arts. Former pupils include poets, pro singers, several bishops, broadcasters with the BBC, president of the Law Society, founder of *Eagle, Girl Swift and Robin*, discoverer and curer of Burkitt's lymphoma, president of Royal College of Surgeons, horticulturists, high court judge, and George Adamson of *Born Free*.

Eastnor Castle

Of the great Victorian castle revivals, one must look at Eastnor and its wonderful look created under a sudden duress: the need to suppress a possible Napoleonic invasion. Wood was necessary for the navy, so the architect employed cast iron for roof trusses in place of large wooden beams. The main materials used included handsome sandstone brought from the quarries in the Forest of Dean by canal and then mule.

Greatly to be admired is the fabulous Gothic Drawing Room and lavish work on a long library and colorful state bedrooms. You will find this in Ledbury, Herefordshire.

THOUGHTS WHILE FLYING HIGH!

Edinburgh Princes Street: March in Joy

Imagine your university's school year coming to an end. And with it are all those heady and cram-filled exams to complete a year of vigorous study—three hours of comprehensive exams for *each* subject for the entire year.

Then it's over. The relief is enormous and leads to an uncommon sense of demonstrative enthusiasm at the knowledge one more school year is part of history—and the end of those dreaded exams. The results will be posted shortly thereafter. But now it is time to show gratitude and exuberance. You can't imagine how well you feel until you join the growing throng and have changed into whatever incredible costume you think represents "you." And then you link arms and walk, march, dance, sing, yell, and fall in love with every lady (or chap) within eyesight.

It's pretty amazing. You are part of one synchronized group for five ruddy blocks and then break off to go to parties or church or wherever your heart and emotions lead you.

Another priceless bit is that the police stop *all* traffic. They arrest no one. There is no overt drunkenness. Old, worn faces along the marching route—haggard from their own pressures—are now alive and full of hope. And even young onlookers along the way smile, cheer, and wave. They seem to feel it is their day as well.

When I was a student, a fellow student wore his top hat, a tuxedo shirt, cuff links, long black socks, and garters. His shirttail was long and mostly covered his knickers (undershorts). I wore my costume from the opera in which I had just starred: *Le Fille de Madame Anjou*. I looked challenging in a French Revolutionary outfit.

One postscript is due: The day ended late with a reverse march back down Prince Street and up the hill towards the university. At the head of this august procession walked the university chancellor and other officials from the school and city. But the key was the honored person who would this day be the most honored man in Scotland. He got a special robe, plumed hat, a staff, and great medallion and chain. And while he spoke in the great honours celebration in McEwan Hall, on the campus, the curious tweaking of Scottish humour interrupted his entire oration with swinging bags of flour, some of fish heads, which opened and covered all participants. This was the same honour afforded Lister, Bell, Fleming, Churchill, and others.

Edinburgh Military Tattoo (Edinburgh Festival)

Each year the Edinburgh Castle Esplanade hosts the great exposition of Scottish infantry battalions, marching pipers, and other displays of precision marching and music. It is all part of the festival (mid-August to mid-September) featuring the overall presence of performers, dancers, singers, international artists, great theatre, music, and opera at *many* venues throughout the city and its outskirts.

English Form of Government

The Magna Carta in 1215 forced King John to agree to the demands of certain feudal barons who wished to protect their rights and the rights of the peasants. It was first passed into law in 1225. The 1297 version still remains on the statute books of England and Wales. This was the first time the people forced their will and sought their rights from any reigning monarch. It was truly indebted to the 1100 Charter of Liberties, which King Henry I passed to limit the powers of the king.

All this, and more, proved to be part of an unmodified constitution. Lord Denning noted: "It was the greatest constitutional document of all times—the foundation of the individual against the arbitrary authority of the despot." Then in 2002 Lord Woolf hailed it as the "first of a series of instruments that now are recognized as having a special constitutional status."

Wikipedia goes on to say: "The charter was an important part of the extensive historical process that led to the rule of constitutional law in the English speaking world."

The government consists primarily of a sovereign, prime minister, and a full bicameral parliament (House of Commons/House of Lords). Everything is done in the name of the existing sovereign, but that monarch has little power to rule or make major decisions.

The sovereign (currently queen; next will be a king) ascends the throne as the head of state, performing constitutional and representational duties. He or she does open parliament in the House of Lords. The sovereign heads all state functions for the Crown, and he makes visits and receives and supports diplomatic persons from other countries. It is also a pleasurable responsibility to undertake ceremonial and official tasks. The queen in the next government does not rule or have any real executive roles, except in those Commonwealth countries where she is perceived as head of state. She may not be involved in politics and must respect the positions of those of other countries.

The king does an awesome job of meeting both the social and cultural needs, even though he is actually a figurehead and not acting executive. This means having moments to commemorate the deeds of others and offer solid awards for distinguished service, often with honours and even personal visits.

Together they may play many roles to support the affairs of state and to give visible recognition to those citizens who distinguish themselves in many different ways, including those serving in the military.

A major part of a monarch's position is seen as Defender of the Faith and Supreme Governor of the Church of England. He helps appoint bishops and archbishops. He is expected to help preserve both the self-governing Church of Scotland and many other smaller but respected denominations and religions, helping to encourage tolerance and mutual understanding.

He also is considered the fount of justice, for it is in his name that law and order must be maintained. He is the head of the armed services, thus receiving regular consultation regarding declarations of war and peace on the advice of his senior ministers.

In time, the fifty-four Commonwealth heads of government will elect a head of the Commonwealth. It is not automatically given to the king and is not inherited. Should the king be elected it will be his prime responsibility to maintain and encourage positive links between all these governments.

He opens and often presides at the Commonwealth Games and even certain other key sports functions. The traditional Christmas Day broadcast will be expected by those who watch TV or listen on the radio, and also for the annual Commonwealth Day in March. At that special date he and his family attend the multifaith service at Westminster Abbey.

As if this wasn't enough, the king and queen depend upon and give leadership to a staff of 1,200 men and women. And they have the same responsibilities at all seven of the royal residences (listed elsewhere in this book).

The prime minister leads by being elected from within his party after a major election (usually every five years) occurs by the electorate for the 650 seats in the Commons. He is the link to all parts of government and confers with the monarch and gets the royal assent and signature on documents.

The House of Commons generally introduces bills, debates them, and sends them to the House of Lords for review and approval. The final vote on most things generally is in the Commons. The House of Lords may also introduce bills for consideration.

The House of Lords has generally been considered key to providing an upper variant as a select committee process to finalize legislation before presentation for royal assent.

Lords are generally gentlemen who have inherited the titles and land, associated with both money and the peerage. It is from the House of Lords that the message from the Throne is always given.

Lords are not elected. They gain their positions by inheritance, by appointment, or through ecclesiastical role in the Church of England. Thus there are two types of lords: lords spiritual (twenty-six bishops of the Church of England), and lords temporal (the rest of the lords, many of whom are appointed for life). The number may vary due to death, resignation, or other reasons. The House of Lords currently consists of 792 members.

Many of the important duties for moving the government forward occur in Whitehall. This includes, but is not limited to:

10 Downing Street (Prime Minister)
Admiralty
Cabinet Office
Department for Environment, Food and Rural Affairs

Department for Work and Pensions
Department of Health
Foreign and Commonwealth Office
HM Treasury and HM Revenue and Customs
Horse Guards (parades and protection)
Ministry of Defence
Old War Office
Scotland Office (Dover House)
Wales Office (Gwydyr House)

You will also find the Banqueting House, the Cenotaph (like the Unknown Soldier), Monument to the Women of WWII, and Trafalgar Studios. Once it also contained Scotland Yard, later moved to the Embankment.

Enigma Code of Heroes

During the Second World War, what needed to be found and retrieved above all else were the Enigma codebooks of the German navy and army. The HMS Petard, a P-class destroyer, was on patrol in the Mediterranean near Port Said (Egypt) on 30 October 1942. With three other naval vessels, it set up a powerful and widespread pummeling of the sea with depth charges. It forced one U-boat, the U-559, to surface. Soon after, the sub's conning tower was hit by a shell, forcing abandonment of the ship.

One of the men noticed that the ship was floundering but still afloat, so he and two others dove into the waters to the tower. Somehow they got inside, found books they believed might be valuable, and one of the men took them and swam back to his ship. The other two men were unable to surface and went down with the ship.

These were the vaunted Enigma codebooks, and they helped mightily in slowing the war and giving away enemy plans and positions. The two drowned seamen were awarded the George Cross for extreme heroism. The other lad was awarded the George Medal. He later died in a fire in 1946.

Eros or Angel?

For many years passersby believed the little naked being with the bow and arrow on the southwest side of Piccadilly Circus to be *Eros*. But the reality is that one Sir Albert Gilbert created this statue to the memory of Anthony Ashley- Cooper, Seventh Earl of Shaftesbury. It is a memorial to his dedication to a deep Christian faith that rose above party politics (the Earl was a Tory). He was devoted to better education, improvements for factory workers, philanthropy, protection of child workers, reform of lunacy laws, and slum clearance. And the answer seems clear: Sir Albert called it *Angel of Christian Charity*. Oh yes, one of the avenues leading into Piccadilly Circus is Shaftesbury.

Executioner's Place and the Royal Mile

St. Giles Cathedral (Church of Scotland, mother church of Presbyterianism) is near the center of the Royal Mile (from Edinburgh Castle, it is one mile to Holyroodhouse Palace). There is a building with a tower on the opposite side of the street. It housed, from time to time, a convict in the high tower, and halfway down lived the man who would prevent his escape and also execute him.

This was the time when Mary, Queen of Scots was held captive in England for almost nineteen years. Her first husband, when she was fifteen years old, was King Henry II of France, who died in a jousting accident. She would return to England and marry her cousin, Lord Darnley. He gave her a son who later became King James I of Scotland upon his mother's death, and later, King James I of England. The son actually deprived Prince Darnley of the right to become king when Darnley was murdered. Shortly after Darnley died, Mary betrothed Bothwell (an unscrupulous advisor) who was threatened by the lords in Edinburgh and escaped to France, only to die in madness in prison, an alcoholic and a pirate.

Fairytale Castle

Everyone has a mental image of how a glorious castle should look. There is no heir apparent in most places, though there are many pretenders. What is clear is that it must have a high vantage point, lots of turrets and battlements, some kind of moat, and a drawbridge. It is romantic but not too attractive until you get close. Start by going to Alton, Staffordhsire, near Alton Towers, the fabulous theme park.

This was the seat of the great Talbot family, Earls of Shrewsbury who literally fell asleep (as in the story of *Sleeping Beauty*). In the 1840s there was an awakening, you might say, by the great Victorian architect Augustus Welby.

The current revival began in 1993 and probably will never end. But it takes time to cover more than eight hundred years of challenging history. You move from a Saxon stronghold right up to Sir John Talbot. The first big link was through Bertram de Verdun, a Norman knight. He built the castle high on the rock and provided the curtain wall. There was a Saxon heiress who married the first Verdun. Her name was Rohesia, and sadly her spouse ran off with Richard the Lionheart on a crusade. He never returned. He is interred in Acre, a victim of the Battle of Jaffa in the Holy Land in 1191. Thus, the castle began a long descent into the hands of women, most of the time. Sir John succeeded him.

The loyal family men battled in such noted places as Agincourt and Bosworth, connecting along the way with Joan of Arc and even Mary, Queen of Scots. At one point Cromwell's men bombarded the castle and left it in fiery ruins. Then a fine architect, Pugin (builder of the Houses of Parliament), helped the Sixteenth Earl of Shrewsbury, and the castle was restored including a new Catholic church, school, and monastery. These remained and grew until 1924 when Alton Towers and the castle were sold, along with thousands of fine acres of land. This was only the second time in the nine hundred years of the immortal *Domesday Book* that this castle was sold.

It would return, rising from more than ashes and crowded history. In 1966 it was established as a Catholic Youth Retreat Centre and attracts many youths to its noble environs. The castle still includes: dungeons, battlements, and high turrets. And it is possible to climb high on the battlements and look down at the roaring River Churnet some two hundred feet below the precipice itself.

You may also visit the glorious chapel with its magnificent, vaulted ceilings and see the recreated Throne Room with its elaborate embroidery, the dais, and the lovely wall hangings. Even John Talbot's sword has been recreated. And close out the experience by watching the light shimmer through the beauteous stained glass windows. Fairytale? Why not!

Falkirk Wheel and Antonine Wall

The Falkirk Wheel is a rotating boat lift in Scotland. For a long time there was a canal in southern Scotland from Edinburgh to Glasgow (Forth & Clyde Canal—115 feet lower than the Union Canal). Union Canal, from Glasgow to Edinburgh, had eleven locks allowing the waters and boats to go to a lower level over a span of 1.5 kilometres (roughly 0.9 mile). Sadly, they never were engineered to meet. They were closed in 1933, and much of the latter stages of the Union Canal were gutted or filled in, making it unnavigable.

The real problem was that these canals could *not* connect. According to Wikipedia: "The difference in the levels of the two canals is 24 metres (79 ft), roughly equivalent to the height of an eight-story building. The Union Canal, however, is 11 metres higher than the aqueduct which meets the wheel, and boats must pass through a pair of locks to descend from this canal onto the aqueduct at the top of the wheel. The aqueduct could not have been positioned higher due to the conflicts with the historically important Antonine Wall."

Thus one barge might come to the end of the canal and loads would have to be carried or transported by hand or trolley or wagon to the other canal.

Wikipedia continues, "The Antonine Wall is a stone and turf fortification built by the Romans (c. AD 142) across what is now the central belt of Scotland. It ran approximately 39 miles and was about ten feet high and

15 feet wide. Security was bolstered by a deep ditch on the north side... The remains are less evident than the better known Hadrian's Wall to the south (in England)."

A whole new plan occurred in 2002, allowing boats and some barges to ply the waters of either canal and be bodily lifted to the other canal, saving time and monies and connecting east to west in southern Scotland. It is truly an engineering landmark. Only a boat lift in Belgium is taller than this one. This wheel is the only rotating boat lift of its kind in the world. You can get on board, take a boat ride for about 1 kilometre on the other canal, and return. There is a charge.

What has this to do with England other than close proximity? Its wheel was designed and constructed by Butterley Engineering at Ripley in Derbyshire (UK). It's worth the trip to see this amazing project.

Farthings: 1279–1960

The last farthing was demonetized in 1960. This coin had fallen in value until it was virtually worthless. It had started as a silver penny and later became copper in mintage. Later, under Charles II, the coins were made with tin with a small plug of copper. Before 1279, when the farthing made its first appearance, it was common to take a silver penny and divide it into two halves or four quarters. Thus it could be said that the name *farthing* may have been derived from the words *fourthing* or *feorling*. Today these coins are a collector's delight.

Ferry: Harwich (UK) to Den Hoek (Netherlands)

It was Christmas in 1955. Still a student at the university, I accepted an invitation from my dear friend Joost Tengbergen, in Gouda, to spend some of the holidays with his family. How I looked forward to going from Scotland to England to Dutch country. We met when he was a Fulbright fellow at Kent State University in the United States. I looked forward to seeing him again and meeting his family.

The ship left the dock at Harwich in very cold weather and choppy seas. We knew it would be a five- to six-hour ferry trip. We were filled to overflowing because of military personnel and other visitors going to Europe to be with loved ones at Christmastime. Many of the lads were imbibing a bit heavily and others milled around because there were few seats available.

About halfway across the English Channel we hit very rough waters and stormy weather. The waves began to mount like towering cliffs and the winds grew fierce and biting. Soon the ship was like a small cork in an active Jacuzzi, and it was very hard to keep one's feet. Most passengers sat down or even stretched out. Nothing was comfortable!

The wind roared and tore the railings from both sides of the vessel. Soon a huge blast of frigid air roared, bursting some windows on the bridge and making it difficult for the helmsman to see and control direction. The entire hull was attacked until the aft sections of the ship were lifted mightily and one of the screws broke loose. We settled back into the deep shadows of the changing waters, only to discover that some of the power and direction control was now at risk. The captain decided to reverse course and return to Harwich. While returning to the home base, many of the passengers became deathly ill. Another passenger and I rushed to the small bar in the back of the main room and discovered lots of paper bags, which we then gave to anyone who felt sick or was already nauseous. Some we held in our arms to quiet and comfort them. Others fell asleep after first expelling drink and food alike. There was one lad, a Dutch marine, who was so ill and drunk that he was lying on the steel companionway stairs to the upper deck, being bounced mercilessly by each wave and lifted and thrown onto his back. By now he was almost unconscious, so we carried him to a flat deck and helped ease him into a less troubled slumber.

We eventually got back to the original port and waited for hours until the ship was repaired and we were allowed to resume our journey. The very ill were removed from the ferry, and we were allowed to stay or go on. Most opted to leave.the ship.

We finally arrived at the Hook (Den Hoek) of Holland, some twenty-four hours after the original departure. It was so good to touch land and to see my dear friend there to greet me. With him were his sterling parents who had survived an enormous ordeal in a Japanese concentration camp in Java during World War II. Here also were two wee lads who had already had one Christmas and were about to receive more gifts from me. You see, much of Europe gives gifts to children on 6 December (Father Christmas Day). Then they go to church on Christmas Day. I rode to church on the back of the bike driven by the mother of Joost and the lads. It was wonderful to give thanks for this safe reunion.

It is noteworthy that Joost became an ambassador from the Netherlands to several different countries, the last being India. Then he was asked to go to Den Hague and be the personal advisor to Prince Willem.

What a glorious coincidence: to be living in the UK, this time in York, England, and looking to the time when Prince William might become king of the United Kingdom. My friend Joost was key to being part of the future of Prince Willem (Dutch for "William") in line to be the next king of the Netherlands.

Flint Mines

It is noteworthy that many Neolithic mines were in vogue as early as 2000 BC, and before. There are at least 360 shafts, of which the best and currently available for discovery is what has been called "Grime's Graves" near Brandon in Norfolk. The residents appropriated antlers from various animals to be used like pickaxes to break loose the hard flint for making weapons, tools, and forms of axes and adzes. They shipped flint all over the English countryside. You can climb down into Grime's Graves (thirty feet by ladder) and see the interior galleries and artifacts.

SIR RICHARD N. DAVIS

The Flying Scotsman

This is a train that has carried passengers between London and Edinburgh since 1862. The East Coast Railway, which now operates the Flying Scotsman, came about in the nineteenth century through mergers and acquisitions. The three main companies—North British Railway, the North Eastern Railway, and the Great Northern Railway—joined forces and the Flying Scotsman became a reality.

It was originally called the "Special Scotch Express," employing same-time departures from King's Cross, London, at 10:00 a.m. and Waverley station in Edinburgh going south to London. That first journey took 10½ hours, which included a half-hour stop in York for lunch. By 1888 the competition and vast improvements in technical services reduced the time further to 8½ hours.

By the turn of the twentieth century, trains had advanced in modern ways to help the engines be more efficient and also to provide more features for the riders. This meant dining cars with full luncheons, and heating, plus an advantage of corridors between the cars. The York stop was cut to fifteen minutes, and the total trip time remained the same: 8½ hours.

In 1923 there was a grouping of railways in Britain, and in 1924 there were four major railways involved. The Flying Scotsman became the firm name for this rapidly moving train that offered much more convenience on board. Part of this was due to the new locomotive, the Greeley A1 Class. The time was reduced to 8¼ hours. The coal consumption got better and used less fuel. There was now an engineer, fireman, and replacement driver, reducing fatigue. In 1928 they steamed north without stopping. The catering improved, as did other services, including a barbershop. And in 1932 the trip took only 7½ hours. This was reduced in 1938 to seven hours and twenty minutes, even though there was now a stop at Newcastle-on-Tyne. This lasted until the first diesel locomotive appeared in 1962. That came about because dieselisation was slowing replacing old steam engines.

On 23 May 2011 the Flying Scotsman brand was revitalized and could make the trip from Edinburgh at 5:40 p.m. to London in exactly four hours, stopping at Newcastle. It is operated by an InterCity 225 Mallard set, Class 91 locomotive 91101. That is only one way. There is a different train to Edinburgh, which takes four hours nineteen minutes. If you desire class, speed, fun, and a great view of English landscape, then empty your piggy banks and have a go!

Follies

What is a *folly* in Britain? Folly is a misunderstood building," according to Headley and Meulenkamp in their book, *Follies*. There are at least 1,500 of these in England, Scotland, and Wales. Some are hard to find. Others are not open to the public. And some are questionable, if only because they are not as clear as one would wish to see. Still, that helps make a folly a folly.

You can learn more about them by reading *Follies: A National Trust Guid*, *Follies: A Guide to Rogue Architecture*, or *Follies and Garden Building of Ireland*. If you really get hooked, then you should join the Folly Fellowship. Then you can be most informed and uptodate.

Here are some "starters," for readers; rather good to see but not necessarily the best. Start with Scotland and then go to England:

Whalebone Arch	Blyth Bridge
Bear Gates	Traquair
The Pineapple	Dunmore***
Folly Lodge	Chapel Rossan
Woodhead Farm	High Valleyfield (B&B)
Fetteresso Church	Stonehaven
Castle Lodge	Thurso
Calton Hill Folly Group	Edinburgh
Scott's Grotto	Ware, Hertfordshire
Portmeirion (Folly Village)	Merioneth, Gwynedd
Rushton Triangular Lodge	Rushton Northamptonshire**
Peterson's Folly	Sway, Hampshire**

Stowe Gothick Temple   Stowe, Buckinghamshire****
Waddesdon (Grotto and Aviary)   Buckinghamshire**
Follies   West Wycombe, Buckinghamshire**
Bell-Turret and Arbour   Castle Combe, Wiltshire
Wentworth Woodhouse   (South) Yorkshire

**Rather Good
***Quite Good
****Among the Best

Headley & Meulenkamp FOLLIES

Foreign Medicine and Doctors

Many travelers fear going into a foreign country and needing a doctor, clinic, hospital, and medications. Little need to worry. The doctors are very well trained, and that's been the case for a long time. Some of them received partial education in the United States. British medical schools are of the highest order.

Many diseases have been analyzed and researched very carefully by astute medical personnel. There is also good news because the medications are often based on the findings and approval of the US Food and Drug Administration. Do not be concerned. You will like their attention, their suggestions, and the fact that quite a few of them still make house calls.

Fountains Abbey Tunnel

You can walk and walk and see lakes, cascades, endless flowers, and gorgeous gardens with all kinds of foliage. There are even little buildings apart from the great ruins of a once superb abbey. Each step brings new vistas and claims attention for the briefest of moments. But then come the water gardens and a most inviting path up the hill to the Octagon Tower. It's a long, winding path edged with old, old trees—some so gnarled and bent they look like the ghosts of yesteryear. When you finally get to the top, you may sit, eyeing this curious tower that may have served many purposes over the years. Now it's closed and only open to the imaginings of each innocent passerby.

Nearby is a dark and solemn entrance of great mystery. No big signs or history to help. There are huge boulders that form an arch. You may think: what is this place and where does it lead? Milady is afraid of the dark and closed places. On our visit I ventured in and saw nothing because there is no light. I scrambled back and urged her to take my hand and together, enter this dark, dark tunnel like the blind leading the blind. Each step was a bit unsteady and there is not even a trickle of light to indicate the other end may be near. Milady squeezed my hand firmly and her cries made me wonder if I had made the wrong choice. Then came the soft hint of golden light. We moved more boldly. A happy awareness flowed through our bodies knowing we were almost back to real sunlight and the end of the tunnel. As we stepped through that last portal, a powerful joy overwhelmed us. We looked to the other side of the hill and saw the magnificence of the gardens, distant birds and other moving objects far below, and the pools of the abbey. We experienced the very glamorous "Surprise View." This is not to be missed, unless you are faint of heart or become easily out of breath from climbing.

You can also look down the other side of this very high hill and see verdant valleys and lazy streams churning their way through natural rocks and trees. When I last climbed, it was hushed by a whooshing sound. I turned just in time to see two military jets roar down that valley at what seemed to be very high speed. As the planes disappeared you could feel a slight breeze and a curious warmth from their powerful jets. Nature was not designed for mechanical interruptions. But it only briefly disturbed the elegance of nature's handiwork. Slowly we descended from this prized place atop a small world to relax, pondering these precious moments.

SIR RICHARD N. DAVIS

The Cerne Giant

This is the incredibly large Cerne Giant, cut from the underlying chalk on the long hillside just outside the village of Cerne (Dorset). Legend has it that barren women from all over England and even other countries journeyed to Cerne to spend one night with the "Giant." They sought to sleep the night on his chalky sex organs, hoping this would make them fertile, ready to have the child they coveted so much. It was destructive to the Giant's image. Authorities were forced to place a fence around his entire body (he is 180 feet tall). It's still there for all to see. However, no more touching is allowed, or sleeping.

Gilbert and Sullivan for One Full Week

Gilbert and Sullivan, English writers and composers, created fourteen comic operettas that featured the humourisms, librettos, plays, and satires that are the calling cards of Sir W. S. Gilbert in the late 1800s. Sir Arthur Sullivan was a true musician, the unofficial composer laureate of England and favorite of Queen Victoria. He also wrote operas and oratorios and at least seven well-known hymns, the most noted being "Onward Christian Soldiers."

Most of the theatrical music since the early 1900s owe a debt of thanks for their songs, choruses, and political tweaking that has touched modern musicals. Their performers were rarely professionals; the satirical points of their offerings were devoted to the gentle embarrassment of the rich, the doughty, and the politicians of the age.

Nothing has been lost in the presentation of these old but richly popular efforts. They are too alive and the words too charming to age:

"I always voted at my party's call/And I never thought of thinking for myself at all."—*H.M.S. Pinafore*

"To gain a brief advantage you've contrived…"

—The Pirates of Penzance

"Instead of rushing eagerly to cherish us and foster us, they all prefer this melancholy literary man."

—Patience

"When next your house do assemble...you may tremble."
—Iolanthe
"Release Hilarion then and be his bride...Or you'll incur the guilt of fratricide!"
—Princess Ida
"Now let's see about your execution—will after luncheon suit you?"
—The Mikado
"In short, this happy country has been Anglicized completely!"
—The Grand Duke

So, as a student at the university, one could see and enjoy *H.M.S. Pinafore*, *The Pirates of Penzance*, *Iolanthe*, *The Mikado*, *The Yeomen of the Guard*, *The Gondoliers*, *Patience*, and *Trial by Jury*. The cost in 1954 was thirty-five cents.

To wit, my favorite London hotel is the new Savoy, next door to the Savoy Theatre. (Do try the American Bar). The earliest part of the Gilbert and Sullivan collaboration began with the purchase of the Savoy Theatre on the Strand. It helped by the creation of the company known as the Savoyards. Later, another group was formed that toured England and many other countries. It is the D'Oyly Carte Opera Company, which still performs strictly Gilbert and Sullivan.

Glyndebourne—Festival of Opera That's Grand

If you love opera, proper picnics, rustic settings, and a distance from all big cities and radio and TV, then you need to dress to the nines and head down from London, east from Bournemouth, or west from Dover. You will find a grand olde house with exquisite design, copious flowers, and meticulously tended gardens. This elegant home has one of the most exotic seven-hundred-year-old roofs anywhere. To top it off, you will hear great— no *grand*— opera sung by superb professionals from all over the planet, eat and drink to your heart's content, and wish this day would not soon end! This place, just short of heaven, is Glyndebourne and is owned by the same people, the Christies, who also bring you these cherished music moments.

It can be reached by train or bus to Lewes and by taxi to the Christie mansion. Car is better, if you have access to one. The road from any angle is fine, and the villages nearby are solidly English. And there are ample places to stay the night or eat other meals than the one at intermission.

Be sure you come equipped with a good picnic hamper, full of your treasured foods and drink. You may be able to get champagne cheaper somewhere else, but it is for sale at the house if you so choose. Bring a throw and/or folding chair(s) for the eighty-five-minute intermission. Allowing decent weather (be sure to bring your "brollie) and enjoy the tall trees and gorgeous flowers, along with their sweet aromas. And you will watch the white, white clouds dancing across the sky, along with a soft blue background. This is spring/summer in England at its best.

Oh yes, the reason you are appearing. You have paid richly for tickets that take time to come available. On *rare* occasion you may be able to call within a day or two for some ticket(s) that were just returned. But don't count on it!

And the whole production, whatever you are seeing, will be well presented. It's a sheer enjoyment to watch and hear. The repertoire includes Mozart, Strauss, Donizetti, and a ton of other well-known and some lesser-known idols.

The key: it is all done well and the whole day is a memory for the ages.

Grampians and Trossachs and Ben Nevis

The very heart and support of central Scotland is wrapped around the **Grampian Mountains**. They are tall and lush, filled with wildlife and incredible flora. They dip from southwest Argyll to the redoubtable coastline near St. Andrews. There are glorious glens, which Angus has in abundance.

To the north are the **Cairngorm Mountains**, six in number. Each is craggier and sturdier than the others until you are overwhelmed by the highest of all, one called **Ptarmigan**. They all rise majestically over four thousand feet into the cool Scottish skies. It is also worth the trip to see the inimitable Cairngorm National Natural Preserve.

Campbell, who annihilated much of the clan of MacDonald at Glencoe, is a place close to the feral areas of **Rannoch Moor** and reaching for the approaches to Angus and Perthshire. Below these are the romantic and flowing **Trossachs**, which were sites of many, many battles, but more to the point, trysting places for man au pair, even to this day, along and close to the numerous lochs that beautifully appear around every turn and embellish these gorgeous hills They are called the "Highlands in Miniature." It is where Rob Roy stood proudly, and with love, for his native land. Even the great bard Sir Walter Scott chose these venues for many an adventure in his powerfully exciting books and verse.

Ben Nevis is the tallest mountain in Britain. It is 4,409 feet tall and attracts in excess of one hundred thousand climbers each year, especially to the tall "ice wall."

Grizedale Forest and Lake District National Park

Those who love nature and want to see natural sculpture and other art forms, as well as magnificent flora and fauna, must hike through this forest. There are more than ninety items carved or cast from wood, stone, and other elements from the earth found in this forest. The views make you feel alive, and the soft breezes and sweet aromas from countless vegetation lend credence to the fact that this is a well-planned and greatly maintained taste of the Lake District.

Towering over Windermere, town and lake, are the soft but slightly steep hills that take time to climb and afford views unavailable elsewhere. You can pause anywhere and sit down, just gazing at the lake and the many forests and wee villages. Then scurry to the top and turn around, marveling that you are now seeing three or four shires in a whole new panorama of awesome delight.

Guardians of the Queen

They were first called to service during the reign of Henry VIII in 1509. There have always been royal guards, but this time they wanted a higher class of men "exceeding in magnificence and expense any contemplated by his predecessors." That from the young king himself.

At first they had "men of speeres," or men at arms, modeled after the plan of French King Louis XI. Listen to this requirement: "This year the King ordered fiftie Gentlemenne to be Speeres, every one of them to have an archer, a demi-launce, and a custrell, and every speere to have three great horses, to attendaunt on his personne."

Demi-launce: foot soldier armed with a short spear

Custrell: sword-carrying attendant

Great horse stallion, no taller at the wither than a pony

To be a bodyguard meant expense and devotion to honour, risk, and duty. First blood was drawn at the curious Battle of Guinegate on 16 August 1513, or the Battle of Spurs. It became disingenuous because the French Cavalry *quit* the field.

From that moment forward, the king wanted them at every formal occasion, the most noteworthy being the Field of the Cloth and Gold. And in 1520 they showed the last known display of chivalry when they took the field at the Battle of Boulogne in 1544.

Until the Civil War they never took to the field again, and only once under the Protector they battled the Scots at the Battle of Pinkie in 1547.

James I, who could not stand the sight of a drawn sword and yet ordered the translation of the Holy Bible into what is now called the King James Version, sought to reduce the guard to what it is today: state ceremonies and court.

William IV, the "Sailor King," armed them and had them "on call" (in English parlance, "stand to.") They needed to fire muskets, but only three could fire but not aim them. Along came the Nearest Guard, as Queen Victoria named them. She insisted on seasoned veterans, of which there were to be no fewer than twelve men who acquitted themselves well, with awards from the queen.

Their weapon is unusual but symbolic. It is the poleaxe. It gets its name from a six-foot shaft holding an axe that is used to crush a pole (a skull). This was, at one time, a fearsome weapon. The uniform is that of a heavy dragoons officer of about 1840.

Their current duties include attending the monarch on all state occasions, including: the opening of parliament, the Garter Ceremony at

Windsor, state visits, great ceremonies of coronation, royal weddings, Jubilee, and at the end of a reign.

Guy Fawkes Day

There are those who wish he had not come from York or even from Scotland. It wasn't that they objected to his attempt to blow up the English Parliament along the Thames. It was his abject failure! All of the gunpowder, the fuses, the watchful sentinels, and the timing were there. But nothing happened. Fawkes was imprisoned for this foul deed against the Crown. Every year there are massive explosions of fireworks on 5 November all over the British Isles to show poor Guy Fawkes how to do it. He did make a mess of it in 1605!

Hailes Abbey

This abbey was created in 1245 or 1246 by Richard, Earl of Cromwell, called "King of the Romans" and also the brother of Henry II. The king gave the abbey to his brother. Cistercian monks came in and built the whole settlement in short order. It was consecrated in a ceremony that involved both the king and the queen and fifteen bishops. This site invited and received many pilgrimages of faith, due in no small part to a special phial of blood that was donated by Richard's son, Edmund. The blood was deemed to be the blood of Jesus, and people came to see and be blessed by such an awesome part of the church. The proceeds of these visits provided sufficient funds for the monks to improve and rebuild.

It was King Henry VIII who had his men examine the blood, and they declared it to be fake. The truth was out and admitted. The abbot refused to give up and would not be a part of the Dissolution Act of 1539. The monks finally did surrender the abbey on Christmas Eve 1539.

Then came the change of one wing into apartments and part of it as a dwelling for the Tracy family in the seventeenth century. All of these buildings were later demolished, and all that's left are a few arches and all the stone foundations for the chapel, the dining area, the monks' quarters, and the laundry.

The rest is beautifully maintained grass and unrestored wall paintings.

It is owned and managed by the National Trust and is very worthwhile to see and experience. You use a small recorder and follow good signage to walk around the entire complex hearing words and sometimes music and even praying and laughter. It makes you feel as if you were there.

Half-Hangit Maggie

Edinburgh has its Grassmarket just below the castle. It is on a road that stretches around the south side and allowed stagecoaches to stop so people could eat or stay the night. There also were those who wished to be transported to other venues, including London.

It was in this area that one Maggie Dickson lived, worked, and took care of her husband. On 1723 she deserted her husband, forcing her to leave the city and move south to Kelso. There she worked for an innkeeper in return for her simple lodgings.

She had an affair with the innkeeper's son and became pregnant. She was so desperate to avoid discovery by the innkeeper because that could mean she would lose her job and her room. She tried everything to conceal her pregnancy as long as possible. The baby was born early and died shortly after birth. She planned to carry the body to the River Tweed and dump it into those waters, but she lost heart and left it on the riverbank.

Somehow when the baby's body was found, it was traced back to Maggie. She was charged under the contravention of the Concealment of Pregnancy Act and taken back to Edinburgh for trial and execution. This took place in public in that same Grassmarket on 2 September 1724.

They took her body down from the gallows and pronounced her dead. Her body was sent to Musselburgh for burial. The sad journey was interrupted by a knocking and yelling from within the wooden coffin.

The lid was lifted. She was quite alive. The law says, even today, that if one is executed and still lives, that person must be freed. She lived for forty more years. A pub in the Grassmarket is named Maggie Dickson's in her memory.

Harris Tweeds May Be in Trouble

Anyone who has fancied one of the finest coats or jackets ever created by the Scots from Harris Island knows they are among the finest handmade tweed garments anywhere in the world. Everything is spun, woven, and made into the jacket, marked by an orb and filled with colored yarns that show the craftsmanship of more than two hundred years. There are no machines—only fine human talent, sewing, weaving, and coloring.

The mill was acquired by outsiders in the last century who felt sure they could manufacture Harris Tweeds by a mechanical process. It failed miserably. In the late 1990s the number of cloths produced approached seven million metres. Today it is down to a mere three hundred thousand metres. The fabric is such that fashion houses are leaning towards more use of it. The need is to inform and energize the buying public so this noble art may be restored and men and women alike may enjoy all the wonderful products that still may be made by these craftspeople. These unique skills are handed down, hard to learn. It is such a unique skill. Its loss could influence others to fall away as well.

Hat, Wig, Powder, and Other Taxes

The late eighteenth century was filled with many unusual improvisations. One was to wear a wig. Another was to have powder for that wig. And the last was most important, being the sign of fine grooming for men, a hat and a cane. Because all these special "goodies" were native to the landed gentry, the king thought it right to tax the wig, and then the powder for that wig, and finally the hat. In 1815 the Wig Tax was a guinea (one pound and one shilling); that's about forty-one pounds today or, in dollars, sixty-six dollars or so. The Hat Tax put a stamp inside each hat, and you were expected to pay for it each year. Failure to do so could create a very hefty fine. And if you made a false stamp and were caught, it could mean a big fine or even your life! Hat makers had to have a license—about two pounds. Outside of London a hat trader paid a mere five shillings. Hat sellers had an official sign in front of their establishment. There was great consternation as to what would be a hat, even if you put anything on your head. It was very confusing, and the act was finally repealed in 1811.

Numerous rulers sought to tax beards. The strongest was from Henry VIII who already sported a beard but never paid the tax. His daughter, Elizabeth I, also taxed beards. Did she dislike beards? Or was she caught up in getting more easy monies from another source deciding to tax windows?

King William III legislated the Act of Making Good the Deficiency of the Clipped Money in 1696. There were too many ideas about income tax and the feeling that no one should know what income any man made but himself.

The king didn't care. Every house was to pay two shillings per year, possibly more, depending on the number of windows. The increases began at ten windows and escalated at twenty-plus windows. They later reduced the numbers, and this rather curious tax met its demise in 1851. It is still possible to see some Georgian buildings in England with windows boarded up so they are not windows!

Charles II was ingenious. He wanted a Hearth Tax because so many people moved around and were hard to find or even track. Thus, every hearth, no matter the number of house occupants, was to be taxed. The tax was one shilling every Michaelmas (29 September) and again on Lady Day (25 March).

The officers in charge of collecting taxes had the right to enter the house and count any additional hearths (such as fireplaces) and increase the taxes.

Then there was the Chimney Tax, which was very volatile. One woman hated it so much she stuffed up her chimney, and the ensuing fire destroyed twenty-five houses and fifteen other buildings and killed five people.

Another curious tax is *scutage*, or *escuage*. If one refused to serve the king and country under Henry I, one could pay not to do it. However, there were some moments when the Crown, Richard I, refused that choice unless the sum of money was big. Edward III was the last monarch to charge this tax.

Hire Cars (Rentals)

Hire (rent) a car for driving in the UK either before you go or once you arrive. There are many choices and sizes. You need to know the differences, from mini to economy to small compact to large compact to intermediate to standard to luxury and even convertibles and SUVs. They may be sized by number of passengers, distance to drive, amount of luggage, and costs.

You also need to know about their charges. Be sure you check with your own insurance company. They may cover your hire (rental) car. If not, you must sign for some insurance, which can be expensive. Be sure to find out if the car has a boot (trunk) or if there is a cover (tonneau is preferred) if you must put any belongings in the back that may be open to peering eyes.

Be sure to know what restrictions are on mileage and if you are expected to fill up with petrol (fuel) before returning the car. Be sure to get a local map. If you do not bring your own GPS (you are allowed to do so), then it might save you time, aggravation, and money if you rented one from the car rental agency.

You need to know if there is a charge if you wish anyone else to drive your car. And be *sure* you get a posting of *all* international road signs from AAA or some other source. You'll be glad you did. And if you have never driven a car on the left side of the road, then be sure to find a big parking lot and make some turns and stops at imaginary places, learning to think *left* instead of *right*. It may save your life.

One other thing about driving: there are many brands of petrol, some of which are familiar in America. Most brands charge alike in an area; the same price is not standard all over the UK. There are basically three octane concerns: four star (premium), unleaded, and diesel. In most cases you only need unleaded, which is less expensive. The cost per gallon will be mind-boggling at first. Just remember each gallon is heavily loaded with taxes. The costs vary per day, and the imperial gallon is essentially 4½ litres, which translates into approximately 1½ gallons. And most cars will use at the rate of 32 miles per gallon or better, city and country.

There is a national speed limit of seventy miles per hour and district speeds throughout the country. Trust them. You probably won't be stopped for speeding (they have cameras that take a picture of you and the car and it is sent to the rental agency) and you must pay to get your deposit back or even to leave the country. The warning signs are of old-fashioned cameras (like reporters used to carry). That means a radar may be in effect just ahead. Why take a chance?

Pedestrians must look right before crossing the street; drivers need to look both ways and think left for oncoming traffic and right for some turns. Here are some car hire companies for your choosing:

Hertz
Hirecars
Holiday
Kemwel
Kendall
National
Net Flights
121
Opodo
Sixt
Thrifty

Use Seat Belts   *Return Home Safely*

Holkham Hall

One of the finest examples of Palladian architecture in England is Holkham Hall at Wells on the West Norfolk coast. Thomas Coke was a man about to inherit an awesome sum of money plus estates elsewhere. He wanted to get ideas about a bright new house he wished to create. His travels led him to Richard Boyle, Third Earl of Burlington (1691753) and his protégé, William Kent (c. 1685–1748). He was a landscape gardener, furniture designer, and architect-to-be. The challenge: create something special amid marsh and heath.

THOUGHTS WHILE FLYING HIGH!

Kent was hired and told something was desired in the Palladian or neo-classical style. Kent approved all plans and stuck to the details. Upon Kent's sudden demise, Matthew Bettingham, a pupil of Kent, was hired. The work began in 1734; acquisitions moved in slowly and finally unpacked. Coke was created the Earl of Leicester in 1744 but sadly died before the house was done.

The hall was central with four wings, all built in yellow-brown bricks from local clay. The remains today are astonishing and without alteration. There are those who term the exterior to be "severe." The north approach is rather forbidding; approach from the south, over the hill past the tall, tall obelisk, and everything falls into place with strong natural aspects and the North Sea in the distance.

There are more than three thousand acres. The land is bordered by stone, which serves as a wall some nine miles long.

When Lady Leicester died, the estate was passed on to a nephew of the late earl who accepted it and changed his name to Coke. He was succeeded by his son, Thomas William Coke. He became quite famous as a great seventeenth-century lawyer and defender of the common law. He became known as "Coke of Norfolk," a paragon among landowners and prolific in the discovery and making of great agricultural innovations.

He made land arable and still had room for sheep. There were unusual and extensive experiments with livestock. The sheep shearings held each year in the barn drew the interest and respect of farmers from miles around, not to mention visitors from Europe who wanted to learn about new ventures in land farming and animal birthing and training. He helped so many become quite wealthy that they chose to create a monument to honour him: the obelisk is as tall as Nelson's Column in London's Trafalgar Square and built two years after the tall honour to Nelson. Here is a bit of trivia for all visitors: there is no statue atop the obelisk, only a sheaf of wheat. The pedestel has a plow, seed-drill, Southdown sheep, and a Devon ox, which refer handsomely to the special improvements made by the earl. Sorry, no carved lions anywhere.

This grand man passed away at age eighty-eight in 1842.

The second earl chose to build an orangery and a north porch. Terraces were laid out along with balustrades in the south front along with the inimitable statue of Perseus and his fountain where he rescues Andromeda from the sea monster. Acres of land were reclaimed from the sea, planting great pines for at least four miles to protect Holkham from the sea. Nothing ever hurt the house.

What awaits inside? The awesome marble hall is one place no lover of real culture and great architecture would dare miss. It reflects a Roman temple, but you cannot mistake glorious decoration and rich trappings for something that would be a grand vestibule to an emperor's palace. The ceiling, the marble stairs, and the fluted Ionic columns made of Derbyshire alabaster are gorgeous. Then there is another saloon with a variegated ceiling and walls hung with Genoan velvet. If you love great paintings, you will enjoy Rubens' *The Holy Family*, Gainsborough's portrait of *Coke of Norfolk*, and a cartoon of Michelangelo's *Battle of Cascina*.

There is a statue gallery for many busts and sculptures from Italy. The library is filled with famous old and later books. And just to add a crowning touch to this very special place, "Capability" Brown did the ultimate landscaping.

Honi Soit Qui Mal Y Pense and the Most Noble Order of the Garter

For those who travel to the UK and have any awareness of symbolism and chivalry, they will be both pleased and confused by the Most Noble Order of the Garter, an order in chivalry that reaches back to the eighth century because of many legends, some myths, and tales of great heroism. But this order came into being around 1348 when Edward III created the order as "a society, fellowship, and college of knights." You either had to be a knight already or be dubbed a special knight for acceptance. The real notions of the origin of the "Garter" are spurious in most cases, but the generally accepted version comes from the Countess of Salisbury and may refer either to Joan of Kent (the future daughter-in-law of the king), or it may have been one whom the king admired: his mother-in-law.

The key to this simple story lies in the fact that the king was dancing with the fiancée of his son, and her garter, while dancing, suddenly slipped to the floor, to the delight and twittering of the many courtiers around the floor. The king, noble and heroic, picked up the garter and tied it around his own leg with the solemn warning: "Honi soit qui mal y pense" (which means from the French in subtle translation: "Shame on him who thinks ill of it").

There aren't that many French words, phrases, or actions employed in Britain. This one makes a bit of sense for the occasion. It was clear enough to encourage, so the story goes, Richard I to be inspired by St. George (patron saint of the English) to tie a garter around the legs of his knights. Edward III presumably knew of the event of his grandfather and fought victoriously, led by the memory of those moments. From this he founded the Order of the Garter.

This is the world's oldest national order of knighthood in continuous existence. It is the prime, the top of all honours for British knights. This order is limited to a sovereign and no more than twenty-five full members, known as companions. Men are "knights companions" and women "ladies companions," though never "dames." There may also be added members from the royal family and some foreign monarchs, known as "supernumerary" knights and ladies. The sovereign alone grants membership to the order.

The garter is the symbol and is a buckled velvet strap worn by men on the left calf and by the ladies on their left arm. It originally was light blue but today is dark blue, and the flowing mantle is lined with white taffeta. It also appears on the emblem. And the full heraldic garments are worn with honour and dignity on very special occasions. With a long blue velvet robe, a hat of black velvet with a plume of white ostrich and black heron feather, a silver shield on the breast, and a gold collar, what could be more magnificent?

Each June all gather in Windsor Castle and, preceded by the military knights, proceed to St. George's Chapel. New knights are installed, and the old knights take their places in the quire (choir), seated in the stall with their name on that stall, and above each knight is his or her heraldic banner with the personal coat of arms.

For the man his banner, helm, mantling, crest (woman: coronet), and sword are always there. All is removed at death. The brass nameplate resides forever in the stall.

The Scottish highest honour is called the Most Ancient and Most Noble Order of the Thistle. The Irish equivalent: the Most Illustrious Order of St. Patrick.

All of these are of the highest honour and supersede notation except for Baronet, George Cross, or Victoria Cross. Nominal letters may also be added to one's name for stationery or public notice, for example.

King Alfred the Great

Most historians seem to agree that King Alfred was indeed the finest of all British monarchs. In fact, no other ruler has been honored by the title "the Great." His birthplace was in a modest palace or villa at the foot of the Berkshire Downs, but it has sadly vanished.

A superb story that may have survived the early years (born 847 or 849) is from his mother, Osburh. She showed a beautifully illustrated volume of Saxon poetry to all four sons and read it to them. She promised to the first one who would be able to read it aloud she would give the book as a gift. Alfred was only six but was the one who did it first and was given the book. The father was Ethelwulf, and Alfred ("Aelfred" in Olde English) came to be his father's favorite.

In fact, he took his son on a pilgrimage to see Pope Leo IV for a blessing to Alfred from his godfather. Thus, King Ethelwulf wanted him to be his successor.

When they returned home, it was found that the eldest son, Ethelbald, had taken over the throne and made himself king. Ethelwulf accepted this rather curious situation to avoid causing a rebellion and then retired to Kent, where he reigned as sub-king until his death in 858. Alfred was then about eleven years old, still studious and growing in determination, intelligence, and resolution, despite the many afflictions that assailed his young body.

Each son reigned as king in his turn. When the youngest was king (Ethelred I), Alfred emerged and stood by his next-youngest brother in the fight against the Danes and their constant invasions of towns and hamlets. At the now famous Battle of Ashdown, in the Vale of White Horse, pious

Ethelred prayed so long in his tent that Alfred chose to lead his troops in a furious assault on the Danes.

Though the battle was won, the young King Ethelred died of wounds sustained in that fight. The Saxon council of wise men then elected Alfred as king. He was a fine warrior at twenty-one, and the other two sons were passed over. At that time there was no such law as primogeniture (next in line by birthright ascends the throne). It was clear he was the best choice.

The attacks by the Vikings increased, and they defeated Alfred so many times he chose to bargain with them and ended up paying them to stop. That bit of tranquility lasted about five years. The Viking army split, one-half marching north to Yorkshire and staying there; the other half made one more attack and then chose to colonize in Mercia.

Still, Wessex was attacked again, forcing Alfred into hiding in the Somerset marshes, waiting for his defenses to be reinforced and to hold the kingdom together.

Alfred had a great love for jewels and other ornamentation. His crown, which is gone thanks to the pillaging and fires from Cromwell, was described as "studded with emeralds." One jewel that survived is in the Ashmolean Museum at Oxford. It is known as the Alfred Jewel.

In 866 King Alfred gathered together all his jewels and other resources and retook the city of London (remember that the first capital, Winchester, was under Alfred). He went on to defeat those Vikings who had fled north, and a treaty of peace was signed at Wedmore. The leader of the Vikings, Guthrum, converted to Christianity, and Alfred was his godfather for that event. Alfred accepted the colonization of much of England. A line was drawn from London to Chester, creating an invisible line that allowed anything north of this to be Danelaw.

The army was well provisioned and ready to battle should another challenge emerge. And they now had a navy with new ships that were bigger and better than those of the Vikings.

Villages grew and the whole countryside was dotted with new and better strongholds, with none of them being more than twenty miles away from another.

Then the king turned his attention to education due to the deteriorating learning in most of England. It moved from rudimentary education to training for nobles and to encourage the scholars to come from afar to learn.

The Royal Court was established to accomplish these hopes, and it became a magnet for scholars. English became the official written language. Alfred translated the works of the Venerable Bede, Boethius, Gregory, Soliloquies of Augustine, and others. He began the *Anglo-Saxon Chronicle*, which was first written in Anglo-Saxon and not Latin. Copies were placed in churches and monasteries.

Alfred established a legal code, thus creating a Saxon law. He limited the practice of blood feuding and imposed heavy penalties on those who broke their solemn oaths and vows.

Most of his life he suffered from an undiagnosed illness. Some said he had seizures. A few said he would fall asleep and could do nothing. Still others described his bouts as depression. And others have opined it was epilepsy.

He died in Wantage at fifty-three years of age. He was buried in the Old Minster at Winchester. Later his body was sent to the New Minster, now Hyde Abbey. Tragedy was to befall even his body. Vandals stormed these special plots, and both religious houses and tombs were despoiled. Many bones got mixed and the end result was a series of caskets with bones, of which some were Alfred's.

A fitting epitaph: "Alfred the King of the Anglo-Saxons, the son of the most pious King Ethelwulf, the famous, the warlike, the victorious, the careful provider for the widow, the helpless, the orphan and the poor. The most skilled of Saxon poets, most dear to his own nation, courteous to all, most liberal, endowed with prudence, fortitude, justice and temperance; most patient in the infirmity from which he continually suffered; the most discerning investigator in executing justice, most watchful and devout in the service of God" (Florence of Worcester, thirteenth century).

King George III and Eton Birthday Boat Procession

King Henry VI founded Eton College in 1440 and helped it off to a grand start. He did unusual things for the school: he gave the school a piece of the Virgin Mary's thumb, a whisper of Christ's blood, and a sliver of the True Cross in hopes it would encourage greater spiritual awakening for the boys. Other than these rare objects, he hardly ever went by or stayed at the school. But the boys felt endeared to their founder. Each day these lads, in their quaint and yet majestic frocks, are expected to pass his statue in the ancient yard, always on the left.

When it gets to be June, you have to think ahead to the fourth. This is to celebrate King George III's birthday, although that is not the real date, and often it has to be moved to another day if it falls on a Sunday. But everyone knows about it and looks forward to many visitors and the glorious walks among the aromatic and romantic gardens seemingly everywhere. The air is festive and the banter does not quit.

Then comes that special moment along the river when the four top rowing crews from the past four years glide past the assembled crowd. Most of the time they all stand, save for the lad in front and the tiller. They are in their white duck trousers, white shoes, blue blazer with the Eton badge on it, and that noteworthy straw hat, garlanded with flowers—fresh flowers—and holding their oars with the blades pointing to heaven as they move those vintage wooden rowing sculls past an excited and admiring crowd.

George was considered a bit "off" by many and sometimes did rather curious things in politics and in the world of his time. But he never stopped going to Eton, dropping in to see student and professor or don alike. Sometimes he even invited one or more to have tea at Windsor Castle. He loved the outdoors and enjoyed agriculture. Some lads even called him "Farmer George."

Well, another happy birthday. Sorry you let the Americas get away?

King George V and the British Empire

This grand monarch was ready for his time. The Great Depression was in the process of unfolding, especially in Britain and in the United States. And this king had a wondrous and loving wife who gave him five sons and one daughter, Mary, The Princess Royal. The first son, Edward

VIII, abdicated his throne to marry the twice-divorced American, Wally Simpson. Then came Albert, who was a stutterer until he was forced to assume the regal throne as king. He overcame much of the problem and married a dear lady who became the darling of all Brits during the Second World War. (Read elsewhere about the Queen Mother).

Mary, the wife of George V, was not the best and warmest of mothers. In fact, it has been said that almost every child cried whenever the mother walked into the room, which usually was for less than thirty minutes each day.

In spite of these factors, and many more, this King George V was a brilliant and powerful leader and ruler. Born in 1865 he had a long reign, passing from this world in 1936. During his rule the English navy, the maritime shipping and the rights to many territories allowed the empire to grow until 62.5 million people were under the British reign as subjects or as members of acquired lands and islands. This was the largest empire ever known in this world.

When George V died, he was succeeded by Edward VIII, who abdicated. Then came George VI who married Elizabeth Bowes-Lyon, the Queen Consort. Together they had two daughters, Elizabeth and Margaret. Elizabeth II is now the longest reigning monarch in the history of Great Britain. In a very special way, she is continuing the wonderful impact and leadership of her grandfather and the great Queen Victoria of the nineteenth century.

Lancelot the Gardener

Not the Lancelot of the Round Table. This incredible man, Lancelot "Capability" Brown, was born in Northumberland in 1716 and began work as a gardener at sixteen years of age. He moved to Stowe, one of the most renowned garden centers in England, and served there until 1749. It was there he began to study architecture, along with his own method of moving and replanting trees. He married in 1744 and began work at Warwick Castle (1749), the castle of kings. He went also to Hampton Court Palace and then Blenheim Palace, where his designs became well-known and he became renowned for planning and planting the trees, shrubs, and floral landscapes that would last and renew for decades.

In thirty-four years he was responsible for the design of the grounds in all the above, plus all of these homes, castles, palaces, and gardens:

Clandon Park	Sledmere House
Claremont	Stanstead Park
Corsham Court	Stowe & The School
Fawley Court	Syon House
Highclere Castle	Tottenham Park
Longleat	Warwick Castle
Luton Hoo	Weston Park
Moccas Court	Wimpole
Park Clandon Park	Wrest Park
Petworth House	Wycombe Abbey

The monument close to the lake at Croome Court states most clearly: "To the Memory of Lancelot Brown, who by the powers of his inimitable and creative genius formed this garden scene out of a morass."

Visit at least one of these gardens to enjoy his great vision and ingenuity.

Longleat and the Safari

Wiltshire is the site of one of the fine "prodigy houses," and it was created by Sir John Thynne (1567–1580). It is also considered a Tudor majesty. It was a place where Elizabeth I loved to visit each summer. Part of this is due to Longleat being the first English country house. It was built for the same family that owns and runs it today. They have added on to the house and gardens, and it was the first house in England to open to the public.

The square elements and decorative exterior are in the Renaissance style with all the major rooms facing outwards. There are many bay windows, reflecting the French château styling. There are little niches for busts and other types of artistry. Cornices run between the floors, and at a roof level there is a balustrade. Look to the top to the domed turrets, which they hoped to use for private, more intimate banqueting. Thynne chose to employ the best Bath Stone from a quarry at Box. Finally, the inner courtyards function only to admit light.

There are eight libraries of which Bishop Ken's library is paramount; it runs along the entire upper floor and has massive first edition volumes.

Of no small consequence: "Capability" Brown designed the gardens and the rest of the massive landscape. The first wild animal preserve outside Africa was created here in 1966. It is the largest non-zoo safari anywhere.

Long Man of Wilmington and Others

This Long Man was carved on the hillside in the prehistoric chalk just outside Eastbourne (East Sussex). Like Cerne it is powerfully attractive and very tall. It may have been the work of the Celts. The oldest known chalk carving on any hillside belongs in the Vale of White Horse above Uffington in Oxfordshire. Some say it may have been created by the Saxon leader Hengist (whose name means "stallion" in German). Others credit it as an honour to the indomitable Alfred the Great who was born nearby. Prehistoric dating would seem to rule out such possibilities. But these "big three" (Cerne, Wilmington, and Uffington) are worth seeing. There are thirteen white horses in Wiltshire and Oxon, and eleven more in other shires (counties). They vary greatly in size, shape, and age.

Mayflower

It was this vessel, some 90 feet long with 20 to 25 crew members and 102 passengers on board the 180-gross-ton vessel, that was burdened by the need to take on the Dutch passengers from the tinier *Speedwell* that had brought settlers to Southampton. They joined forces and sailed to Plymouth.

On 16 September 1620, the *Mayflower* disembarked Plymouth and headed to Virginia. Between terrible storms and bad navigation, they ended up going around the tip of Cape Cod, dropping anchor off what is now Provincetown, Massachusetts. A special party was dispatched to find an amenable site for the new colony. While on board the passengers discussed and voted on the governance of this new venture. History now calls it the Mayflower Compact. It was the first form of constitution in the new world. The honored few included John Alden, William Bradford, William Brewster, John Carver, Miles Standish, and Edward Winslow.

It was mentioned earlier that a ferryboat went from Harwich (UK) to Den Hoek (Holland) at Christmastime (1954). The *Mayflower*, built and sailed from that same Harwich, toted supplies to France and Holland. For about two hundred years, royal men-of-war were built there for the Royal Navy. It is still a prime harbour.

Mazes

They are not alike in size or composition, though all invite adventure and uncertainty, even in getting lost. They are made of hedges, walls, and some natural materials, including rocks and streams. Some are man-made and mysterious. They all are entertaining and a tad fearful. You discover by walking, crawling, getting lost, needing help. Some say these are among the best:

St. Bees Maize Maze, north of St. Bees village
Cairnie Fruit Farm, Fife
Chatsworth, Derbyshire
Hever Castle, Kent
Hampton Court, Surrey
The Forbidden Corner, Yorkshire
Maze World, Warwickshire
Longleat, Wiltshire
Jubilee Maze, Herefordshire

Mermaid Street (Rye, Sussex)

Rye is the English name for whiskey, but the well-known name of Rye also applies to a town by that name in Sussex on the east coast of England. It is about two miles from open sea and a part of the bay that leads to the English Channel and the French mainland.

It is truly a part of a civil parish though its roots reflect a town. It is not large, some four thousand or so inhabitants, and its primary industry at one time was building ships for the Royal Navy and others. Its history is also dotted with smugglers and malcontents. In fact, at one time there was a huge group known as the Hawkhurst Gang who used many inns, including the Mermaid and the Olde Bell Inn, connected by a secret passageway.

All this lent itself as attractive to tourists and a place for an open village to enjoy and nearby water to visit. Today there are ample places to stay, eat, and shop. You can also be involved with the fishing fleet and enjoy yachts and other vessels in Rye Harbour.

You will truly enjoy the charm, beauty, and olde-world feeling when you walk that cobbled street called Mermaid. There are some olde gaslights, many places to grab a nosh or even a grand cup of tea. And the swift salt air will cleanse your nostrils and prepare you for great food and a lovely night.

Metropolitan Cathedral of Christ the King (Liverpool)

This cathedral is unique to Liverpool and to music. First, it is a very contemporary church with a glorious interior and is "in the round." The entire mass takes place in a circular sense and it intends to involve all people, most of whom are closer to the altar than in a conventional nave. Second, it was the site of the premiere of the symphonic mass by Paul McCartney, one of the Beatles. This church is across from the university and not too far from the fine olde Anglican Catholic Cathedral.

Murals and a Statue at Blenheim Palace

For a number of years, visits and learning have been available from Blenheim Palace, the seat of great lords and ladies and the birthplace of Winston Churchill. The grounds were originally designed by Henry Wise, the first duke's gardener, then greatly amplified and made gorgeous by "Capabaility" Brown, who made a lake, the cascades, and vast shrubs and trees. It was later tended by the great Achille Duchêne. There have always been many fine works of art and artifacts and well-trained wardens to help guide visitors into a better understanding both of the palace as a home and its resident treasures.

A number of years ago there were full paintings in tall frames, covering the entire walls of several key rooms. Each huge painting had many, many people in each presentation, including special cats and dogs of various sizes and shapes, all of them part of these families of the caring and serving people who labored diligently at Blenheim for many years.

On my visit a lady warden gave a short glimpse of who the staff were and why they were in these multiple paintings. It seems that Lady Randolph, great-grandmother of Churchill, was the closest friend of then Princess Anne, who ultimately became the Queen of England and all territories (1702–1714). They played together, learned together, and were privy to the discovery of multitudinous niches, crevices, hidden spots, and secret compartments in the palace. They were very close, dear friends.

One day, in their teens, they got into an argument about something seemingly trivial. It grew into a fierce argument and sadly led to the young princess ordering Lady Randolph to leave the palace and take her entire family with her. They were sent away by week's end, never to return during Princess (later Queen) Anne's short lifetime.

When Queen Anne died at age forty-eight having birthed seventeen children, only one of which lived for even a few years, the Churchills and Randolphs were invited to come back to live in the palace, which they did. Then occurred the most incredible and meaningful events of those difficult years. Lady Randolph got permission to have three huge wall paintings created (noted above). They contained actual visages of everyone who worked at Blenheim, including the animals. She wanted them to be thanked and remembered.

She had one more thing to do to honour her wonderful friend, now deceased. She hired a young Italian sculptor to create a statue of the late queen. His artistry allowed the queen, who had become a bit corpulent from her many years of illness and childbearing, to look somewhat youthful, trim, and composed. And from the same piece of stone he carved a scepter and orb in her hands, crossing her bosom, plus an awesome crown, not dissimilar to the one she wore. It was also from the same stone. The statue was placed at the intersection of the Great Hall and the Long Library. It is now in the central part of the library itself and is worth a visit. You will even discover the finely cut stone looking like real Queen Anne's lace at the end of each sleeve.

This had to be one of the finest and noblest moments for any castle, palace, or stately home. What a glowing tribute from an exiled friend who truly cared.

Musicians of Note (British)

This is not an exhaustive list, but it does cover some of the great British composers since the seventeenth century and a bit before that:
Henry Purcell
John Rutter
John Patric Standford
Thomas Tallis
John Taverner
Jeremy Taylor
Sir Michael Tippett
Sir William Walton
Sir Andrew Lloyd Weber
Samuel Wesley
Ralph Vaughn Williams
*George Frideric Hande
One from Italy; the other from Germany

National Memorial to the Few

Among the finest of World War II were the courageous young men who belonged to flying clubs around Britain. They were not trained to fly combat missions and had no access to fighter planes. The government did have fifteen Spitfires, and most were airworthy. The pilots were trained by the Royal Air Force (RAF) and fought valiantly against overwhelming odds against the German Luftwaffe (air force). It was a series of staying battles that bought time to build aircraft, and teach men to fly and fight with the fastest, most maneuverable aircraft in Europe.

Capel-le-Ferne is the solitary place where a lonely flyer (carved in stone) is seated on a large stone, made also as a seat, looking at the channel to watch the boys come back from a bombing raid. This stunning memorial has the names of more than three thousand airmen who gave their lives in World War II as they helped stop the Nazi juggernaut, which was looking to invade and overwhelm the Brits. It never happened. And these dead have not died in vain. Go see this place. You may be there on a lucky day when a single Spitfire flies low over this serene and hallowed spot.

The National Trust

Since 1896 there has been a National Trust, dedicated primarily to the preservation of heritage. This includes the purchase of many buildings and parks and other spaces including castles, palaces, stately homes, abbeys, and access to some cathedrals, not to mention gardens, parts of some coastlines, and even tracts in the countryside. The most unique and rather large purchase was the town of Lacock (Wiltshire) with a population of one thousand-plus persons. It includes a churchyard, museum, abbey, police station, and even a pub!

The Great British Heritage Pass was a most economical and helpful purchase for any traveler to Britain. It allowed access to more than six hundred of these inimitable places either owned or managed by the trust. You pay for specific numbers of consecutive days at a cost far less, in most cases, than the normal admission charge to that project. It is even less if you are a senior citizen and/or traveling in a group. It gives you directions to enable easy routing to each place, something to discover, and sometimes, an opportunity to stay in a castle or other noble venue. (Sadly, this great pass is no longer available after 115 years!)

This trust has not only preserved all the above-mentioned sites, but also the incredible contents, such as fine art. In the aftermath of the Second World War, there was a vast hiatus of art from Britain to other countries. Some believe the losses were caused by high taxes, forcing some estate owners to sell their valued possessions to pay the excises. It was estimated that as much as one-third of this valuable legacy left the country, hurting the worth of the highly valued property, buildings, and other treasures. The bleeding, for the most part, has stopped. Most buildings and art that were in jeopardy are now safely in the hands of the trust, either through management or via newer generational ownership.

No. 10 Downing Street

Just as the White House is home to US presidents, so Number 10 Downing Street is home to the prime minister of Great Britain. This has been the proper home for every prime minister since 1730. In that year, the first one, this special house was occupied by Prime Minister Robert Walpole, who refused to accept the house as a personal gift. He insisted it be given to future First Lords of the Treasury.

This has been the seat of deep planning, urgent conferences, and many governmental secrets. It is a busy office for the prime minister and his employees and also the home for the prime minister and his family. It has undergone many new and valued improvements. It is now a fine residence for the most powerful politician in the country.

This nerve center for two major world wars and the scene of horrid riots, very passionate protests, and other surprises is still the heart of decision making.

(Read about some previous prime ministers elsewhere in this book.)

Olde Customs and Traditions

Ancient times produced many unusual and key practices that have evolved into both great fun and tradition, mixed with some unbelievable artistry and humour. Here are some of the best-known practices that are still happening:

January: Wassailing at Old Mill Farm, Bolney, Sussex. The event also includes "apple howling" to drive out evil spirits with aid to the good spirits to help provide an abundant crop. (First Saturday)

Fitie Wassail, East Sussex. This celebration includes a torch procession, bonfire, food, haystack stage, and a dance floor. (Second Saturday)

Performance of *Twelfth Night*, London and many other venues. This comedy remembers the Magi and Christ. One of the most notable venues is the Globe Theatre on the Bankside in London. (New Year's and throughout January)

Straw Bear Festival, Whittlesey, Cambridgeshire. This festival features a parade, a man dressed in straw in the streets, and dancers. (Weekend near Plough Monday)

February: Hurling the Silver Ball, St. Ives, Cornwall. At 10:30 a.m., the mayor throws a silver ball from the steps of the parish church into the waiting crowd. It is passed along via the beaches and through the streets. The person holding the ball at noon gives it to the mayor at Guildhall and earns five shillings. (First Monday after Candlemas)

Shrove Tuesday. Activities include pancake races in many places. Pancake Grease occurs at Westminster Abbey, where boys wait for the school cook to toss a huge pancake over a five-metre pole. The boy getting the largest piece gets a cash bonus from the dean of the abbey. Some places may also ring the "pancake bell." (Day before Ash Wednesday)

Ash Wednesday. Carry an ash twig in your pocket or sock on this day. You may get trampled if you don't have one! (Day after Shrove Tuesday)

Kissing Friday. English schoolboys, until the war in the 1940s, were allowed to kiss a girl without punishment or rejection. (First Friday after Ash Wednesday)

March: Tichborne (Hampshire) Dole. On the Feast of the Annunciation (Lady's Day) until 1796, a dole of flour was given to the poor. Now the money goes to the church instead. Children receive oranges and lemons. (25 March)

The River Thames used to be wider, and barges brought oranges and lemons to a landing spot just below the churchyard of St. Clement Danes on the last day of March. Primary school children gathered to recite "Oranges and Lemons," an old nursery rhyme. Some would sing the rhyme; others would create an arch that other children would walk through until the rhyme got to "chop, chop, chop." One would be caught by a falling arch and would then choose a lemon or orange and someone to stand behind. At the end was a fierce tug of war, and all received lemons and oranges.

April: There are pax (peace) cakes for being neighborly and sharing, Palm Sunday brings small biscuits (Herefordshire) stamped with the image of the Paschal Lamb and the words "God and Good Neighborhood," and the Easter season brings hot cross buns in Smithfield and the Hot Cross (Easter} Bun Ceremony in a London pub in Bromley-by-Bow. In this ceremony each year a sailor hangs another hot cross bun to commemorate a poor widow who baked a bun for her only son who failed to return from the sea. (Easter season)

Nutters Dance, Bacup, in the Pennines. Folk dancers dress in black with bright skirts and darkened faces and dance through the entire town. (Easter Saturday)

Hocktide Tutti-men, This is in Hungerford. In the fourteenth century, Prince John of Gaunt gave rights to the commoners: free grazing and fishing to locals. This is still celebrated after six hundred years. They have no mayor, and the constable is an elected senior citizen. There also is a portreeve, a bailiff, and the court of feoffees. On this special day, the town crier blows his horn, and the convening court elects the officials and two "Tutti-men," each carrying a tall, tall pole adorned with many flowers tied by ribbons. On top is an orange. The procession winds through the streets, and many women get kisses from the hardy lot. They receive an orange as a thank-you gift. (Second Tuesday after Easter)

May: Chimney Sweeps Festival, Rochester, Kent. The chimney sweeps will be after the chimneys, but not before dancers and musicians have their presence enjoyed. (First weekend)

Spalding Flower Festival, Peak District, Derbyshire. This festival. Late April and early May, features thousands of tulips adorning floats in a masterful parade of flowers. The wells are dressed with ingenious pictures, creations, and colorful decorations.

There are endless customs: beating the bounds, Stilton cheese rolling (Stilton, Peterborough), Furry Dance (Helston, Cornwall, on 8 May), and Padstow Obby Oss, which is the oldest May Day celebration and heavily done in Cornwall. There is also Oak Apple Day, bread and cheese throwing, a wool sack race (Tetbury), and Jack in the Green Festival (Hastings, East Sussex).

June: Dickens Festival, (10-15 June) Rochester, Kent. All participants dress in period costumes and parade in the streets with stories, songs, and dancing, commemorating the time that Charles Dickens lived and wrote there.

Midsummer Bonfires, Cornwall. A long string of bonfires is lit on many, many hills from Lands End in deep southwest to Kithill, near the border of Devon. This celebrates the arrival of summer and the longest day of the year.

July: Oyster Festival and Blessing of the Waters, Whitstable, Kent. The blessing opens the long festival. It highlights St. James Day (25 July), the patron saint of oysters and their fisheries.

Swan Upping on the River Thames. Each year the queen's swan keeper and the designated swan markers row in skiffs to find and mark (brand) the cygnets (baby swans). This is beautiful to watch. (Last Monday)

World Toe-Wrestling Championships, Bentley Bridge Inn, Derbyshire. (Late July) They lock toes together and try to force full foot down. Happening since 1976.

August: Scarecrow Festival, Kettlewell, Yorkshire. Incredible life-size scarecrows are created and displayed around the village.

St. Bartholomew's Bun Race, Sandwich (24 August) This race is run by children around the church of St. Bart's and the hospital. They receive a bun for the run.

International Hop Festival, Faversham, Kent. This festival celebrates the hops (brewery backed) harvestIt occurs the end of August or the first few days of September,

Bog Snorkelling Championships, Waen Rhydd peat bog (near Llanwrtyd Wells in Mid Wales). Contestants swim sixty yards in the peat bog with flippers and snorkel, competing for the fastest time This occurs in the last week of August and are done in deep, thick bogs..

September: Abbots Bromley Horn Dance, Staffordshire. The dance is performed by six "deer-men" wearing reindeer horns. Then comes a dance for ten miles performing rituals in twelve different venues and around the village. The music is supplied from a melodeon and a triangle. (First Monday after the first Sunday after 4 September)

Church clippings, various churches. This involves the many parishioners and others joining hands and surrounding the church as thanks for their blessings.

Horseman's Sunday (third Sunday), St. John's Church, Hyde Park (London). The vicar of the church welcomes horsemen and blesses them. He then leads a bevy of more than a hundred horses and their riders to the church for a presentation of rosettes. (Third Sunday)

October: Pearly King Harvest Festival, (first week) Church of St. Martin-in-the-Fields, London. This festival is quite unique because it is a Cockney tradition started by a young lad who chose to cover a suit with pearly buttons to gain attention and to raise monies for the poor at all kinds of charity events and fairs. Other parts of the city decided to follow this lead, and the festival continues today to benefit the less fortunate *and* to show the glory of London in a stunning display of unusual garb and bright coverings.

Punky Night. (last Thursday in October) This night is not unlike the American carving of pumpkins into jack-o'-lanterns. Once the pumpkins are carved, the children place candles inside, and light them, and march through the streets singing songs, calling at friendly houses, and competing for the best "punky."

November: Soul cakes, West Midlands. *Halloween* comes from the words *hallowed evening*, referring to the special night when ghosts and spectres are banished and the new day regales the saints of old who have made life better by being special "souls." During this time soul cakes are taken to each door by children. They are exchanged for gifts of sweets, pennies, and words of good fortune. This tradition still is practiced in the West Midlands, covering Coventry up to Leeds and Sheffield and over to Manchester. (1 and 2 November)

Bonfire Night has been mentioned elsewhere in regard to the twitter at the ineptness of Guy Fawkes and his sodden gang who failed to ignite the explosives to blow up parliament. So, on 5 November each year there are bonfires, fireworks, and other incendiaries showing Mr. Fawkes how to be "explosive."

The Devil's Stone, Shebbear, near Holsworthy, Devon. Another item of interest on Guy Fawkes Night is in the village of Shebbear. The people turn over a six-foot-long stone under an old oak tree. No one is sure how the stone got there. Perhaps the devil dropped it when he was fleeing from St. Michael, having been thrown from the portals of heaven.

Tar-Barrel Racing, Ottery St. Mary, Devon. This area was famous for its tar barrels. So now the townfolk race through the streets carrying flaming wooden barrels of burning tar on their backs.

December: Mummers Plays, various venues. These special plays have long been a part of English tradition and folklore at Christmas. The plays are early pantomime and owe some of their origin to the legends of St. George and the Dragon. They follow the themes of old morality plays: pitting good against evil. Worth seeing!

Christmas Day Swim, various locations. Many swimmers in dozens of locales get into quite unusual and fancy dress to brave the cold waters nearby for a "bracing" Christmas swim. Locales include Hyde Park, Brighton Beach, Sandy Bay, Tenby (Wales), and Aberdeen (Scotland). (25 December)

There are other traditions in December: Nippy Dipper Boxing Day Dip in Aberdeen; Grantchester barrel rolling in Cambridgeshire; the Haslemere run in Surrey; beach football in Scarborough, North Yorkshire; Maldon mud races at Essex; New Year's Eve swinging the fireballs in Stonehaven in the Grampians (Scotland); and, finally, men in costume carrying burning tar barrels on their heads to the community market centre bonfire in Allendale, Northumberland.

Boxing Day occurs on 26 December all over England. Legend has it that Boxing Day began in many of the stately homes. The day after Christmas there were many prezzies that had been sent by high and noble figures from faraway places and even within Europe. Some were repeats of the items already owned by the recipients. Others were items that were either unwanted or not needed. Thus, on Boxing Day those items were placed in the same boxes, or new ones, and given to the many loyal workers at that stately home or castle.

There also was a "Christmas box" for good luck on ships. It had a slit so the sailors could place coins in it during the voyage with the plan that these monies would be distributed to the poor. It also was the start of the alms boxes in churches and other special places to ensure aid to needy members of that area.

Many of these customs persist today. Thousands of good people have been very generous, whether they were wealthy landowners or hardworking folk.

Oliver Cromwell's Last Hurrah

There is no clear distinction of the vast values of Oliver Cromwell's actions versus the incredibly dangerous and challenging choices he made and carried out. It is clear that he dabbled in Puritanism early on but did not join the movement until later in life. It is also clear that he, among many others, opposed the monarchy and led the "Roundheads" against the "Royalists" in a long series of civil war battles. The end result: the imprisonment of Charles I and then the beheading of this king in 1649. The leadership was in shambles, with deep squabbling over how and with whom the country should be led.

Enter Oliver Cromwell, Lord Protector of England. He fought battles against the groups who opposed him, and imprisoned and even executed others who were not in favor of the England *he* envisioned. He led his country back to a respected status once again. And he burned as many of the crown jewels as he could find. There were also foreign skirmishes as well as key men and women who lost political favor; their lives were challenged and changed forever. Some said he died from natural causes; others opined he had a streak of malarial fever from his foreign encounters. Whichever the cause, a brilliant general and honest dictatorial type died at fifty-nine years of age. He had refused the kingship and, at his demise, he seemingly was given proper burial in Westminster Abbey. He apparently was disemboweled and then embalmed. There is confusion as to what happened then. It is known the body was removed and the head cut from the corpse and placed on a pole atop Westminster Hall, so said Samuel Pepys at that time. It later was removed or blown away.

Finally the remains were found in Tyburn and the head rejoined. It is believed those remains now lie somewhere in the anti-chapel of Sidney

Sussex College, Cambridge, with no rights to discover or disentomb this body again.

There is a statue of Cromwell in front of parliament. In this one he looks almost swashbuckling with his right hand grasping the hilt of his sword, which is touching the earth, while leaning away so his arm is straight out without the sword. He is actually carrying the Bible in his left hand and staring directly at anyone who would challenge him.

In Tyburn there is a larger-than-life statue of Cromwell, dressed in his Puritan hat and leathery boots, along with his sword at his left side, sheathed, and a huge, much-used Bible under his right arm. His left hand has a clear finger pointing at someone or something as if to give firm directions.

At the top of a nearby archway are the sculpted heads of Charles II and Henry II with Queen Anne slightly above. Cromwell's sculpted head is in a side niche.

Opera in Edinburgh

One is always honored to have the leading role in any opera. I was honored to play such a role in an opera that was a cross between satire and humour: Molière's *La Fille de Madame Anjou*. It was sung in English. Most of the cast came from the University of Edinburgh.

The opera, like others written by the Frenchman, was very delightful to read and sing. We were rather rank amateurs, and the timing for a full week's show was not good. Why? It was time for the COMPS (final exam for a complete year of study—three hours for each course). But we tried. My female partner, both good and attractive, sang well. We did our best to be French provocateurs and slightly revolutionary. The rest of the cast deemed us to be snooty and over the top. I couldn't blame them; we were caught up in exams as well as opera.

They had their day (night, actually). When the last curtain came down, the cast plastered faux beards on our chins and removed ugly hats, replacing them with gruesome wigs. We bowed graciously and laughed heartily.

One little side note: a pretty young lass occupied a front seat every night we performed. Each night an additional lass would come and sit with her until the entire front row of seats was filled with young and beautiful secretaries. And they waited at the stage door to thank us! The special grace: the critic said the one saving feature of this musical monstrosity was the fact that the tenor was loud!

As for these young ladies, they invited me to tea one afternoon. As for the exams, I passed with flying colors. And the Divinity School named me the Prime American in the college. Brits and Scots are very special.

(A Few) Painters (British): 1700–Present

Anthony van Dyck	George Gower
Peter Lely	James Thornhill
Godfrey Kneller	Jonathan Richardson
William Hogarth	John Wooten
William Hoare	Allan Ramsey
Joshua Reynolds	Richard Wilson
Thomas Gainsborough	William Marlow
George Romney	John Hamilton Mortimer
William Blake	Henry Raeburn
Thomas Lawrence	Arthur William Devis
John Crome	Thomas Phillips
Joseph Mallord William Turner	Edward Armitage
John Constable	George Frederick Watts
William Holman Hunt	Albert Moore
Dante Gabriel Rossetti	Frank Cadogan Cowper
John Everett Millais	Spencer Gore
Edward Burne-Jones	David Bomberg
William Morris	Mark Gertler
James McNeill Whistler	Alexander Mark Rossi
Edmund Blair Leighton	Walter Sickert
John Singer Sargent	Lawrence Alma-Tadema

Peas on a Knife

Have you ever tried to eat with your left hand even though you are right handed? You *must* be able to do this to be a good Brit. One evening my fiancée drove me to a fine inn at the town of Pickering (near the Yorkshire Moors). It was a late meal, as precious time was spent discovering some of the beautiful spots of that area. I was served a bit of bangers and mash (sausage and mashed potatoes) and some peas. I did well with the first two but struggled with the latter. Finally, in jest, she suggested I place them on my knife and pick them off one at a time with lips or teeth. Just to get them on the knife was daunting; to get them to my mouth was a lost cause.

Finally, she suggested corralling them with a fork (left hand) and then helping them on to the fork with the knife (right hand) mixing mashies and peas and crushing them against the knife. It is hard to tell which succeeded the most—the few peas finally consumed or the growing laughter as she watched abysmal failures.

One must learn the efficiency of using both hands and feeding with the left.

Prime Ministers of Note

Sir Robert Walpole	Second Earl Grey
William Pitt the Younger	Edward Smith-Stanley
Sir Robert Peel	William Ewart Gladstone
Benjamin Disraeli	David Lloyd George
Robert Gascoyne-Cecil	Ramsay MacDonald
Stanley Baldwin	Margaret Thatcher
Winston Churchill	Tony Blair

SIR RICHARD N. DAVIS

The Proms

There is no end to the grand rounds of culture that invade and delight thousands of people in London. One of the finest and longest of musical offerings occurs at the Royal Albert Hall and is known as the Proms. It was founded in 1895 and now consists of more than seventy concerts plus the chamber concerts at Cadogan Hall, additional Proms in the Park events across the UK on the last night, along with associated educational and children's events—which rushed past one hundred last year, for the first time in the sense of classical concerts and musical festivals. Jim Belohlavek has described the Proms as "the world's largest and most democratic musical festival."

Proms (promenade concert due to be outside in pleasure gardens) allow free strolling and casual movements during concerts. That makes seating cheaper than those seats that must be reserved and akin to those who choose to stand inside actual building venues.

The original impresario was Robert Newman, who was responsible for the first indoor concerts in Queen's Hall (Langham Place), seeking to attract those who may not be devotees of true classical music but would still be likely to buy tickets to one of these many concerts because they are less expensive.

A great help early on was the financial backing of a very noted doctor who chose to underwrite the presentations after Joseph Wood was hired as conductor. They became known as Robert Newman's Promenade Concerts. These helped to create a growing interest both in the Proms and also in funding future concerts. There were struggles during World War I and after, partly due to the anti-German feelings that had grown heavily. It took larger organizations to come to the aid of the Proms. In 1927 the best possible assistance arrived: the BBC, which is housed next door to Queen's Hall, took over the running of these classic programs and the future brightened immediately. The BBC withdrew support at the start of World War II in 1939. Bombing and other problems ultimately erased the Queen's Hall as a venue for the Proms. The death of Wood in 1944 meant going in a new direction with a need for very committed professionals. These included

Sir Malcolm Sargent, Julian Herbage, Sir Adrian Boult, Edward Clark and Kenneth Wright, and William Glock.

Contemporary and avant-garde composers were attracted, and soon the Proms invited Boulez, Berio, Carter, Ligeti, Lutyens, Nono, Tippett, and others. It also turned heavily to the past with music from Bach, Hayden, Purcell, Monteverdi, Byrd, Palestrina, and many others. Most compositions were directed by such notable conductors as Stokowski, Solti, and Giulini. It also meant that most of the world's greatest orchestras, and great musicians, both singers and instrumentalists, would come to these choice venues easily and often.

There is hardly a great symphony that has not appeared. And many of the finest operatic soloists have graced the stages for many years. There also have been items offered as lunchtime concerts and even things that meant a fervent collaboration between the musicians at the Proms and the BBC. Promming is still quite evident with more than a thousand standees paying to watch and listen while standing for an entire concert. There are even some standing outside and listening because some windows and/or doors may be open.

And then there is the Last Night of the Proms. It generally has happened on the second Saturday in September and is broadcast on BBC 2 and then BBC 1. The concert is lighter than most concerts, employing a number of well-known and beloved classics followed by a series of patriotic pieces in the second half of the concert. You might hear Elgar's *Pomp and Circumstance* no. 1 and Wood's "Fantasia on British Sea Songs," which might segue into Arne's "Rule, Britannia." The final piece has traditionally been what some call the British second national anthem: Parry's "Jerusalem," and finally, "God Save the Queen."

You will see the people rise and sing lustily for both final pieces. The Prommers have added a piece, not in the program, "Auld Lang Syne." You will hardly find more joy, powerful music, and gracious but jubilant singing than on that last night. There are many, many requirements to even qualify for any available seats on that last night. One is: you must have purchased at least five concerts plus an application for the Last Night Concert and bring the stubs with you! There are many more little things that happen, and it would take a bit of learning to find a way to see and hear what is most valuable to you. It's worth the effort.

Pulteney Bridge (Bath)

If you've been to Firenze (Florence), Italy, and have seen the Ponte Vecchio (a bridge over the Arno River), then you know how beautiful and very interesting the Pulteney Bridge in Bath really can be. These are two of the most attractive and unique structures in the world. And they are similar in that they both have shops on a river in a gorgeous city.

The bridge is named after one Francis Pulteney, who was a wealthy heiress to the Bathwick estate, which was across the river from Bath. There are only four bridges in the world like this, each with shops on each side of the driving lanes. This was first to be a Palladian design, as so many buildings were employing in the eighteenth century. It was designed and completed by Robert Adams and lasted for twenty years. Then they chose to change some of the shops, and the façade suffered from a sheer loss of decorative appeal and dignity. Floods near the end of the century tore up most of the north side of the bridge. It was rebuilt, but not to the same elegance as the original. Part of the difficulty came from shopkeepers changing some of the windows. In 1903 the western and southern pavilions were demolished to allow widening of the lanes, and the recovery was not a true match.

It can be viewed with real pleasure. The best viewing spot is the Parade Gardens park by the Crescent Weir.

The Queen Mother

Elizabeth Bowes-Lyon was the wife of King George VI. She was also the mother of the current Queen Elizabeth. The Queen Mother was actually the queen consort when she became the wife of Albert, Duke of York. He ascended to the throne due to the sudden abdication of his elder brother, King Edward III.

She will long be remembered, after the death of George VI in 1952, for her many gifts of caring. During WWII she was known to venture into smoking ruins after fierce bombing in London. What a sight to see this lovely lady of the Crown seeking to find and help some of the wounded and displaced Brits who were victims of these attacks. She wore her broad brimmed hats many times and was properly dressed as if going to serve tea. The sight of her thrilled all the many who saw her: subjects in distress, and wardens, police, firefighters, and medical corps as well. Her deeds ran through all Britain like wildfires, and her pictures on the front pages reassured old and young, wealthy and poor alike. As Churchill once said, "She was the soul of Britain. She gave us all courage and hope!"

A little moment in later years at Buckingham Palace gave a clear sign of her gracious and loving manner.. It was terribly cold and the lads who stood so proudly and always erect at their guard posts held up the best they could in the blasts of cold air and snow swirling about garments and guns alike. She looked out the window and saw one lone lad whom she feared was freezing and without help. She opened the window and called out to him, identifying herself so he could look up from his post. She asked if he was all right. "Yes, ma'am!" "Could you use a spot o' tea?" "Yes, ma'am!" "Hold on for a few moments."

In a quick flash she had her servants gather some scones and biscuits and a pot of tea and some cups. She had them sent out to each of the guards on duty. And each man, after sipping his hot tea and eating a sweet tasty, looked up and saluted with his gun. She yelled down: "God bless you!"

In most of her adult years her teatime included a fine gin and tonic. In 2002 she died in her sleep, at age 101. England, and the world, will not soon forget her.

Rapeseed Oil (UK)

These crops are much like turnips but are grown for their oil and for the wonderful things that the crops do for the soil. It is not good to grow them too many times in the same field. Two-thirds of all of the oilseed rape is run through a special process in the UK, and the valued oil is the result. It has many uses, none of which can be used for vehicles. The very bright yellow flowers appear in April in great amounts on many farms and lands. They are truly gorgeous to see, especially when the wind makes them wave boldly.

SIR RICHARD N. DAVIS

Ravens at the Tower of London

This is one of the strangest and yet longest legends in British history. It all started with a medieval chronicler, named Geoffrey of Monmouth. He was in the middle of quite a few omens, tales, myths and legends, especially regarding the Welsh. He wrote a book, *Historia Regum Britaniae* (History of the Kings of Britain). He talks about a very early British king called Bran Hen of Bryneich (c. 485). The Welsh word for *raven* is *bran*. An ancient king in the Dark Ages was killed in battle and had requested that his head be buried, as a talisman against invasion, on Gwynfryn (White Mount), which is where the Tower of London now stands. The legend states that if the ravens ever leave the Tower of London, the White Tower will tumble and a great disaster shall befall England.

King Charles II may have been the king who decreed that at least six ravens must be kept at the tower at all times to prevent disaster. He had been told that the ravens were interfering with the astronomical findings at the Royal Observatory, housed in the northeastern turret of the White Tower. The king ordered the ravens killed and then was warned of the apparent "curse" upon the tower and all of England if the ravens were gone. He rescinded the order and said there must be at least six ravens at the tower to help prevent disaster.

There is a ravenmaster who is chosen from the Beefeaters, the Yeomen Warders. The ravens can be vicious and only respond to the ravenmaster. He must take care of their needs and their feedings at all times. He takes them to his home and "hand rears" them for at least six weeks. They generally live for twenty-five years but have been known to live as long as forty-five years. One wing is clipped from each bird to prevent it from flyaway. The ravens live in the Wakefield Tower and are kept at the Tower of London at the expense of the British government.

Rhododendrons and Redwoods

They grow very rapidly as flowers, bursting into bloom in June. They line the road and reach for the skies. Sometimes, this mile and one-half trail in the New Forest has rhododendrons so high they begin to lean and can sometimes reach across the trail and touch each other as if to make it look like a giant tunnel of towering flowers and huge trees, including two tall redwoods (the only ones in all of Great Britain). New Forest is near Bournemouth and also the redoubtable Beaulieu Palace and the great National Motor Museum, which contains more than 250 vehicles from 1895 to the present day. It is the largest museum of its kind in the UK.

There is a similar display: the Laburnum Arch in Bodnant Gardens, Wales.

Robert de Bruce: (1274–1329)

This very noble warrior and hero was of Norman descent, coming to Scotland in the thirteenth century. His grandfather had claimed the Scottish crown when the throne was empty. King Edward I of England claimed a form of feudal power over the existing Scots and then turned the reins over to one John Balliol. This didn't last because Edward decided to imprison him and lead the country directly.

In a sense, that seemed fair because the Bruce clan did not like Balliol and yet gave "fealty" to King Edward. There came the time of the Great Rebellion, and Robert disagreed with his father who chose to back the English till his demise in 1304. Robert joined up with Wallace (another great Scottish hero) and with one John Comyn, former enemy, to become the Guardians of Scotland. A truce came about between Bruce and Edward to avoid Balliol from regaining power.

When Wallace died, Bruce killed Comyn in a church in Dumfries. Comyn was a nephew of Balliol and the slaying by Bruce proved he wanted to be king. Indeed he rushed to Scone and was coronated and crowned Robert I on 25 March 1306. But Edward had many troops around and soundly defeated Bruce on a number of occasions, even killing three of his four brothers and imprisoning his wife, so Bruce chose to hide in Rathlin off Ireland.

He returned in 1307 to Ayrshire and with his brother Edward fought to regain lost lands and people. It helped that King Edward died that year and the son, Edward II, was rather weak. It helped Bruce's cause, along with the support of the leading figure in the Church of Scotland. He defeated another Comyn and then captured the crucial port of Perth from the English garrison stationed there. By 1214 he had captured Edinburgh. Then he joined forces with Philip de Mowbray, who held forth from Stirling Castle.

The two had seven thousand armed men and faced the armies of Edward II at the key Battle of Bannockburn. They employed bogs, gorges, and sloping terrain so that the English could not deploy properly on the narrow front; the spearmen of Scotland held firm. Edward II took five hundred knights to beseige Stirling, and Mowbray signaled surrender and yet would not allow the king to enter the castle.

It became clear that the English were at a great loss after the Bannockburn devastation. The Scots even captured Berwick and ravaged other border towns. Edward II chose once again to recapture Edinburgh but met a scorched earth defense, which forced starvation and retreat. When Edward II had been deposed, the Scots and Englishmen created the Treaty of Northampton, and all claims to Scotland by England were dismissed forever. It was time for Bruce to take hold of the reins of government and bring back efficient leadership. He also found ways to restore lands to those who had lost them to the English. It was a new and drastic change to the place of families and of power in Scotland.

It is believed Bruce died from leprosy or some severe ailment that had not been diagnosed in Scotland at that time. He was succeeded by his son David in 1329. Bruce wanted his body to be interred at Dunfermline Abbey and his heart removed and buried in Melrose Abbey. He had always wanted to go on one of the Crusades to the Holy Land. It never happened. Sir James Douglas took the heart of Bruce, placed it in a special capsule around his neck, and went on a Crusade. He only made it to Spain, and both his body and the heart of Bruce were returned to Scotland, where the heart finally found relief and eternal repose—as one of Scotland's greatest heroes.

Royal Ascot

There are many moments of great gatherings and wondrous acts that fill people with love and admiration forever. Such a place is the site and instance of Royal Ascot. It is a yearly renewal both of fine horse racing and the spectacle of outlandish and ornate clothing and enjoyment of very precious libations in absolutely comfort-filled seats next to all the nobility of the day. This is more than a moment—it is more than three hundred years of a unique heritage and a very solid tradition.

It happens every June when those who can afford it gather in their best dress and rub shoulders with horse lovers and the grand peerage that loves moments of sheer opulence. They sip champagne and attend sumptuous receptions with all kinds of aperitifs, appetizers, and tongue-warming meals, often with five courses.

This jubilee of great racing lasts for one full week. Be sure you understand that these people share with all the greats, including the queen and her family. It is also the time when the finest horses in the world compete for the largest prizes in horse racing, amounting to some $6.6 million.

The queen and her entourage arrive each day with a great entry fit for such royalty. They come in horse-drawn carriages and are escorted to the Royal Enclosure, which is one of the very honored enclosures. It is difficult to get close to these very unique places. Entry to see and bow to the monarch is not totally impossible, but you must have come to these races for four consecutive years or more, be an existing badge holder, and then have a representative of the queen offer an invitation. And you must adhere to a very demanding dress code: men must wear morning dress and the top hat (never the bowler hat) and women must wear whatever the precise needs set for dress before royalty for that year.

Be sure that originality and creativity are the hallmarks of female fashion. The Thursday meeting at Ascot is Ladies Day, and that's when you will experience fashion and styling beyond most other times and events during the year. It covers everything from toe to head, most especially the English love of unique and incredulous hats. It's also the day of the Gold Cup. The queen presents it to the winner, allowing both a meeting with Her Highness and also to keep the cup as his own. Other winners during the week must return the trophies. The race and the course itself grew because of the enormous delight previous regents have taken in watching and enjoying horse racing. It is extra special with the queen because she and her family not only appear, but they also have owned and raised fine steeds that have done well.

The course itself took on new dimensions when it was closed from 2004 to 2006 as major and truly glorious renovations occurred. It is both massive and quite ultra-modern. It is highlighted by full hospitality features that are state of the art and are so futuristic that you marvel at the ease of clearly seeing all the horses run the laps clockwise (yes, from right to left). The center infield is gloriously maintained green grass, and myriads of flowers seem to come from almost everywhere. It cost the equivalent of more than $307 million.

The grandstand is the length of the course and goes past the far turns. All is enclosed in brilliant aluminum and endless glass that makes it all seem open. This is sheer opulence and pure enjoyment.

Thanks to Joe O'Neill, *This England*, Summer 2011

Royal Tidbits

c. 765—The First King of England, Offa, marries Cynethyth, with church approval.

12 July 1543—Catherine Parr becomes the sixth and last wife of Henry VIII, the most married royal.

28 July 1683—Queen Anne marries Prince George of Denmark. Despite giving birth seventeen times (the children all died very young or in childbirth) she left no heirs. Curiously, her best friend was Churchill's great-great-grandmother, who was Blenheim Palace. (see *Murals and a Statue at Blenheim Palace*) by then Princess Anne.

10 February 1840—Queen Victoria chooses to wear white as her wedding dress, a habit that continues to this day.

26 April 1923—A commoner, later to be called "Queen Mum," weds the future King George VI. (See *Queen Mother* in earlier vignette.) Their wedding cake weighed a sumptuous eight hundred pounds!

11 December 1936—Edward VIII abdicates the throne (to his brother Bertie, who became George VI, who stuttered and was trained to speak plainly), to marry the twice-divorced Wallis Simpson.

20 November 1947—Princess Elizabeth weds Philip (a prince from Greece who later became the Duke of Edinburgh and Prince Philip). Elizabeth had met him when they were eight years of age.

6 May 1960—Princess Margaret marries Antony Armstrong-Jones on TV—a true royal first.

29 July 1981—Lady Diana Spencer is the first royal bride in English history to omit the word *obey* from her wedding vows to Prince Charles.

29 April 2011—All trash bins along the route to Westminster Abbey for the wedding of Prince William to Catherine (Kate) Middleton are sealed to prevent bombs from being placed inside, and all roofs along the route are covered by police snipers. The wedding was paid by the royal family, and security was paid by public funds, costing an estimated eight million dollars.

Thanks to *Reader's Digest,* May 2011

St. Bartholomew-the-Great's Priory Church

This church is located in London at West Smithfield and dates back to 1123, established by Rahere, a prebendary of St. Paul's Cathedral and later an Augustinian canon. The tale tells us he erected the church after recovering from a severe and dangerous fever. This helped create a sense that this church was a center for curative powers. Sick people came and filled its aisles each 24 August, St. Bartholomew's Day. It started as a priory next to a hospital. The hospital survived the Dissolution, but nearly half of the priory was torn down. They even got rid of both the nave and all but the last bay. The choir and crossing survived. The entrance to the church goes through a small entryway. It is surmounted by a half-timbered Tudor building. Parts of the cloister survive and contain a small café. Very little remains to suggest any monastic influence.

The church was not ravaged by the Great Fire of London in 1666 but fell into disrepair. The church also was undamaged during World War II. It had been restored and rebuilt in the late nineteenth century, and later restorations have helped bring back much of the old church. The Lady Chapel was once used for commercial purposes, including the one-year apprenticeship of Benjamin Franklin as a journeyman printer. One transept was a blacksmith's forge. Through all of this it was still linked to the hospital, earning the title of "Great St. Bart's." There is an unusual oriel window that once was used by William Barton to spy on the monks, or so the tales state.

You will enjoy knowing that this venue has been home to some fine cinematic offerings: Four Weddings and a Funeral; Robin Hood: Prince of Thieves; Shakespeare in Love; The End of the Affair; Amazing Grace; Elizabeth: the Golden Age; The Other Boleyn Girl; and Sherlock Holmes.

The church also housed the chapel of the Imperial Society of Knights Bachelor until 2005. St. Bart's is the adopted church of various livery companies and is the setting of their annual religious services: Worshipful Company of Butchers, Worshipful Company of Founders, Worshipful Company of Haberdashers, Worshipful Company of Fletchers, Worshipful Company of Farriers, Worshipful Company of Farmers, Worshipful Company of Information Technologists, Worshipful Company of Hackney Carriage Drivers, and the Guild of Public Relations Practitioners.

There is a haunting about a monk who is looking for a sandal stolen from his tomb. And it was near this place where so many were executed during Mary Tudor's reign. Sometimes the night air is infected by the smell of burning flesh.

St. Mary's Student and His MG

The lad was a tall, strapping, good-looking chap from Philadelphia. He started out at Union Theological Seminary with a view to becoming a pastor. He got married to a lovely young lady from Philadelphia whose father was a big importer of Oriental rugs. The wedding present from her parents was a bright red MG convertible. The young man had been accepted as a second-year divinity student at St. Mary's College, the divinity school of St. Andrews University. The new couple settled down beautifully in this old, old village, and they rented a lovely old home just outside the town and high up on a hill. It had to be a special treat for the townspeople to watch each morning as this seminary student came flying down the hill in his red "cut-offs" (student robe) as it flew behind him as if he was caped. And it made the MG glisten even more in the Scottish sun. Was that the devil or was it Paul the seminarian?

Savile Row Tailors

The art of designing, measuring, and creating fine suits, coats, jackets, and other men's finery is known as *bespoke tailoring*. There are very few places choosing to make suits this way. Among the best in Britain are those who are on the single short street known as Savile Row, between Vigo Street and Conduit Street, close to Piccadilly. It is in Mayfair, three short blocks from Old Bond Street.

"From Nelson to Churchill, the great and the good have been visiting tailors on Mayfair's Savile Row since the 18th century," Hilary Macaskill quotes Kathryn Sargent, first female head cutter at Gieves & Hawkes, 1 Savile Row.

"It takes time, patience, and precise accuracy to put inner lining on a man, pinning it to be sure of correctness and allowing room for movement. A light paper template grows from this planning. It includes coat/jacket and trousers. Then it is removed and basic sewing begins. When the shell is finished the cloth may be cut from those templates. The client is then asked back and he tries it on, making sure all is well fitted. Finally, several days, or even weeks later, the client returns for the last time. He tries on the suit, makes sure it is to his taste, with the final approval of the tailor. One can get bespoke tailoring for less than $2,000, but it probably won't have the quality or tailoring finesse of Savile Row."

Seaton's Miniature Tram

Old trams, especially somewhat miniature trams that are big enough to carry passengers, are not easy to find. This one is a narrow gauge railway of all of three miles, and it had to be changed later to a wider gauge. The cars were purchased from another town that chose to stop the services.

The trams are double-deckers and run smoothly along the River Axe Estuary. It is one line with a passing lane near some of the stations. Visibility is excellent and the cost is fair. You can find these unique cars in Seaton and Devon and take the full ride to Colyford if you wish. Upon arrival you may choose to walk out into the lovely Devon countryside and feel the soft breezes and discover many wildflowers growing in profusion and trees galore.

The man who started this healthy mania was Claude Lane, who also knew how to keep the electric power going because he designed the special batteries used to propel each tram. The main terminus is in Seaton, and you are able to experience the lovely sea just one hundred yards away, not to mention turning towards town for some choice shopping.

Shute Barton Manor Home (Devon)

There were not many manor houses in the Middle Ages that looked and acted like fortified castles, only smaller versions. The believed date of this building is around 1380, though it took well into the sixteenth century to complete. Even so, part of it was torn down in the seventeenth century, but the image and major building still stands in Shute, near Axminster, in Devon. What is left is the kitchen and the largest Tudor fireplace in all of England, spanning some twenty-four feet.

The Great Hall also survived and so have the turrets and the late Gothic windows. You will be greeted by the Tudor gatehouse. The family of Pole once owned the building and land. It was also in the family of Lady Jane Grey. It is now owned by the National Trust. Family descendants still have the right to live there.

Songs in a Town Hall

Several times each week when I was living in Edinburgh, a long black car picked me up from my "digs" to go sing some place. Often it was for the Moody Bible Institute and took place in a number of churches. Then it changed.

It was never clear who the benefactors were. The chauffeur couldn't or wouldn't tell me, even though there was no pay for these numerous gigs. No matter! If one loves to sing, this is a superb outlet. Sadly, the many places we were taken to perform were unknown. I often wondered where we were in lower Scotland!

One night the black car went to a town hall, apparently in the heart of the mining district. We were a group sent to entertain men who never saw sunshine, or their families, for most of six months. They went into the mines in the dark. Each mine was dark. And when they came out of the mines night had fallen, often as early as 3:00 p.m.

Of the dozen or so acts that evening, there was only one American, the only university student. He was expected to sing one song and be done. Fine! Looking out, past the large carved tins that served as shields for the huge candles that acted as stage lights, it was hard to look up. One was blinded temporarily by a huge Klieg light that shone right in the face, covering the entire body as well. The house was full. Every seat taken. People standing along the walls. Some seated on the floor of the aisle, and still others in the open area just before the stage. It would have been an American fire marshal's nightmare!

They were hushed and attentive. No instruments, not even a piano. Singing was a cappella (unaccompanied). I chose to sing American songs.

As the first song ended, the applause was deafening. It was a stunner!

They finally stopped. An encore was begged. Again the happy applause. How can seven songs be sung and loudly cheered seven times? There were other acts waiting. A bargain was made with them: one more song and then the other performers must be allowed to offer their talents. Give them their moment and after the planned show ends there will be more songs for anyone who wishes to stay. The last performer did his bit. This seemed to be the finale. Wrong! Not a person had left. So, more songs were sung for over thirty minutes. It was time to part. Some came up and shook hands, others gave a hug, and some a kiss.

It is a part of stage life to act and sing. But those ruddy Scots offered an incredibly warm and lasting welcome. One never forgets such golden moments from such a great audience.

SPORTS (British): Cricket, the "Gentleman's Game"

According to Ask.com, "Cricket is a bat-and-ball game played between two teams of eleven players (substitute fielders [only] are permitted in cases of injury or illness) on an oval-shaped field, at the center of which is a rectangular 22-yard-long pitch. One team bats, trying to score as many runs as possible while the other team bowls and fields, trying to dismiss the batsmen and thus limit the runs scored by the batting team. (A bowler bowls to a batsman. There is a paler strip called the "pitch." There are two sets of three wooden stumps which are the wickets. The two white lines are the creases). A run is scored by the striking batsman hitting the ball, running to the opposite end of the pitch and touching the crease there without being dismissed. The teams switch between batting and fielding at the end of innings…In professional cricket the length of a game ranges from 20 'overs' of six bowling deliveries per side. Test cricket is played over 5 days."

Cricket was first played in England in the sixteenth century. By the eighteenth century, it was deemed to be the national sport. In the nineteenth century, it had spread abroad so there were now international matches.

The key to these matches comes from the bowler trying to hit a wicket and thus dismissing the batter who was to protect the wicket and hit the ball safely towards one of the fielders. A team can win the match by the number of wickets.

This means that if the team has reached the winning target with a certain number of batsmen still left, it has won the match. Thus, if there are ten batsmen and three have been dismissed, then the game is won by seven wickets.

There are many places to see a match all over the English countryside. Thanks to Ask.com, 26 September 2011

Rugby

This game is more like American football than soccer. The legend states that in 1823 in the town of Rugby, England, a lad picked up a ball and ran towards the opposition's goal line. Almost two centuries later, this has become one of the most popular sports anywhere. It is a game in which one team (fifteen players) must get to the other side's goal line and push the ball across and down it for a "try." A try is worth five points, and a penalty try may be awarded if the man carrying the ball is impeded improperly in his forward movement. After scoring a try, there is a conversion, adding two more points. Penalty tries are three points. A player drop-kicking the ball through the uprights scores three points.

The field (pitch) is one hundred metres long with an in-goal area (between the goal line and the dead-ball line), which is twenty-two metres long. The field is seventy metres wide.

There is a kickoff to start the game. It comes from the center of the halfway line (midfield) and must travel in the air at least ten metres. The other team may not be closer than ten metres from the opposing team.

The ball may be passed *backwards* to any player on his team or lateraled with a distinct sign of back-throw, however slight the difference. Any man may kick the ball to the opposing team or sideline if his teammates are behind him. Failure to do this means a scrum awarded to the other side.

If a player allows the ball to be dropped, or rebound off an arm or hand and the ball goes forward, then a scrum is awarded.

Tackling of the man with the ball is allowed by one or more tacklers, forcing the opponent to one or both knees on the ground. He must release the ball at once. This makes for a free ball and can be chased by any player.

A ruck happens if the ball is on the ground and one or more players from either/or both sides are near the ball. They may close and kick the ball to the team's hindmost foot, and it can then be picked up and toted forward.

A maul occurs when the ball carrier is held by one or more opponents and his own players, and the ball is off the ground. The team in possession tries to drive its opponents towards the opposite goal line, and the ball can then be pulled up or dropped and picked up and passed to a player not in the maul.

There is such a thing as offsides: a player too close to the goal or ahead of the player with the ball is offside. There is no penalty, but he cannot play with the team until the ball is declared onside and moving forward.

A scrum occurs after certain penalties and has eight opposing players from each team lock arms and move their feet. The opposing player throws the ball into the middle at their feet and then waits for it to be kicked out, at which time he picks up the ball and tosses it to a teammate.

The game is divided into forty-minute halves with a break in the middle. There are no timeouts, and time may be added if a player is injured or needs special attention or must be removed from the field. This is the only time a substitute may be allowed unless for tactical reasons. Seven men may qualify.

Their equipment is simple: rugby shirt, rugby shorts, socks, cleated shoes, mouthpiece, shin guard inside the stocking, and a nonrigid shoulder pad. The ball is elliptical and slightly wider and longer than an American football.

Soccer

Soccer(football) is a team sport that depends on skill and teamwork. It is two teams of eleven men (goalkeeper included) who play against each other for a total of at least ninety minutes, plus injury add-ons and overtime, to see which one can score the most goals against the other team. Soccer is seen by more people than any other sport in the world, and it's called "football" (futbol) in most places.

The forwards (strikers) play nearest to the opposing team's goal. They have the main responsibility for scoring goals. There are usually three strikers per team. The centre forward is also known as the target man, the one to receive long passes and "hold up" the call as teammates get closer. The striker is better known for cutting off defenders and running into space on the defender's blind side, than receiving the ball for scoring opportunities. He can shoot with either foot with both accuracy and power. He can even slot the ball (kick towards the goal) for breakaways.

The second striker is known as a deep-lying forward who can back up the other two strikers, blend in with the wingers, and help create a goal for a midfielder. All players must be able to defend against both onrushing opponents and stop shots on goal for any number of angles.

Penalty shots are called for serious offenses. A less serious offense may cause a yellow card to be displayed by the referee as a warning. A second yellow card will earn a red card and immediate rejection, with no substitution, and the team will continue to play at a disadvantage of a lost player.

Stained Glass Angels in the High Octagon of Ely Cathedral

There are thirty-two angels in stained glass panels that are movable. They are high up in the octagonal lantern in the center of the cathedral. You may have access to their backside by taking a tour that requires climbing a tall ladder to the roof and walking across to the only octagonal tower in any cathedral in the world. You move behind the panels, some of which may be open, and can see the full lantern and the nave well below your eyes.

Standing Stones in Britain

Avebury Stone Circle—Created around 2500 BC, these massive stones surround and run through the village of Avebury. There is a question about the origin, although, like Stonehenge, there is the thought of a religious significance. Many stones were broken or cast away by superstitious natives in the 1800s, because they presumed there had been pagan sacrifices involving these stones. You can drive through the village, past each stone.

Castlerigg Stone Circle—Keats described it best: "a dismal cirque of Druid stones upon a forlorn moor." They overlook Skiddaw, Helvellyn, and Crag Hill in northern England.

Long Meg and Her Daughters—Near Penrith in Cumbria are the remaining fifty-one stones from the Bronze Age. These stones are in a circle, and the name may have come from a local witch in the early seventeenth century. The area is marked by examples of megalithic art, such as a cup and a ring plus a spiral and rings on concentric circles.

Maumbury Rings—This Roman amphitheater, which started as a Neolithic henge (stone that may overlap or overhang), is just west of Dorchester (Dorset).

Merry Maidens—This is a Bronze Age circle of stones said to have been nineteen girls turned to stone for dancing on Sunday. This is in southeastern Cornwall.

Rollright Stones—Five miles west of Great Tew (Oxfordshire) is the circle of seventy-seven smaller stones known as the King's Men, the last remains of a Bronze Age burial chamber. The stones have a Round Table effect for knights or other dignitaries, with a larger stone at the head of the circle, which could signify some kind of chieftain or even a king. It's all amidst tall trees.

Stonehenge—This is a world-famous structure, built rather slowly, starting in 3000 BC. The stones came from across the Severn and maybe partly from Wales. It is still a bit of a mystery how those people got the stones across the river *and* up the long, sloping hills to the eastern end of the Salisbury Plain. Because of the size, shapes, and positions of the stones, it is assumed they may have been used to track sun and seasonal movements to set calendar and the worship of the sun. Centuries later the stones were used by Druids in their cult worship.

Stone of Scone

There is hardly any rock or stone that has been around as long as the Stone of Scone and with such powerful meaning. It trails back to the great Celtic kings and heroes. They called the stone "Liath Fail." The greatest of all Celtic heroes was Cúchulainn, who split that precious rock with his sword (Excalibur?) when it failed to roar under Riabhdhearg, the legendary high king of Ireland. Legend has it that it never roared again, save for Conn of the Hundred Battles.

Liath Fail means "the speaking stone" because it named the king it would soon enthrone and might sing or roar with joy when he sat on it!

At Scone the coronation stone was "reverently kept for the consecration of the kings of Alba" and "no king was ever wont to reign in Scotland unless he had first, on receiving the royal name, sat upon this stone at Scone, which by the kings of old had been appointed to the capitol of Alba." The Stone of Destiny (The Liath Fail, and the Honours of Scotland" Michael R. Burch

The coronation stone was used to inaugurate Scottish kings going back at least as far as Kenneth I (Kenneth Mac Alpin "the Hardy" or "the raven feeder"). He was the first king to unite the Scotti and the Picts, two warlike tribes in 843.

In 1292 King Edward I of England overwhelmed the Scottish clans by taking the stone from Scone and placing it beneath a new throne in Westminster Abbey. The chair was named after Edward's namesake, Edward the Confessor, England's only canonized king. So now it became the Stone of Destiny, symbolic of England's destiny to rule over Scotland.

All British sovereigns since 1308 have been seated in King Edward's chair at the moment of their coronations, with the exception of Queen Mary I, whose chair was given to her by the pope. John Balliol was the last Scottish king to be crowned on the stone in 1292 and defeated four years later by Edward I.

When Queen Elizabeth I died, King James VI of Scotland became the king of England, thus uniting England and Scotland. Hence each king or queen of Scotland must also be king or queen of England to be crowned on the stone.

King Edward III promised to return the stone to the proper owner, Scotland.

It just never happened until Prime Minister John Major in 1996, with the approval of Queen Elizabeth II, arranged to have the stone properly returned.

However, there was a curious incident on Christmas Day 1950 in London.

Four Scottish lads somehow invaded Westminster Abbey, entered the throne room, lifted the throne chair, and retrieved the Stone of Scone, which is large and heavy. They placed it in their car trunk, sped back to Scotland, and deposited it in the Arbroath Abbey. About four months later, it was found and returned to England with the proviso from the queen that henceforth it would only be used for coronations on a borrowed basis and then returned.

It was used again in England for the formal coronation ceremony of Queen Elizabeth II. The story could end there save for one small footnote. The Scottish Nationalists like the queen but have deep animosity towards the first Queen Elizabeth because of her imprisonment of Mary, Queen of Scots and her subsequent execution. So, when the new postboxes were erected in all of Scotland, they were red with the gold seal of Britain and the letters *QE II*. They took umbrage at this and took rasps and erased the second *I* from each box.

Styling Examples in History

Tudor—Montacute House, Somerset: longest gallery of its kind in Europe. Sixty Tudor and Elizabethan portraits and a timber-framed moated house. Moreton Hall, Cheshire: from 1450. Elizabethan murals, glass, and pewter.

Georgian—Clandon Park, Surrey: inspired mansion of the Palladian medium. Great eighteenth-century furniture, porcelain, and textiles. Osterley Park, Middlesex (near London furniture by Robert Adams, a great designer.

Victorian—Cragside, Northumberland: spectacular top-lit drawing room with Renaissance-style marble chimneypiece. Knightshayes Court, Devon: the finest surviving Gothic Revival houses with superb tenth- and twentieth-century paintings.

Twentieth Century—2 Willow Road, Hampstead: a modernist house full of clever design and a collection of modern art. And you may wish to discover Upton House in Warwickshire with a red and silver art deco bathroom and a vaulted ceiling covered in aluminum leaf.

Teahouse (Coffeehouse) in Edinburgh

If you go one short block north of Princes Street, on St. Andrews in the city there is what looks like a wee alley that goes to the left. You only have to walk a few paces before you see a huge set of steel girders standing on end with a curious building at the top, covered with many windows and reached by a circular iron staircase that suddenly leads into this coffeehouse. It is simple, quaint, and filled with the smells of coffee brewing, a rather unusual twist in a city that adores fine tea.

Students went there often and helped urge many other students to discover this unique place to sip, read, and discuss all kinds of interesting topics. We discovered their food offerings were light and suggested they offer hamburgers. They were astonished, for in the 1950s hamburgers were purely American, and the fine beef needed to make them was not easily available.

So, they bought some good beef and found some rolls (bams) that could serve as buns, and we helped them create a modest stove top that would allow conversion to the needed hot plates with fire beneath to make fine hamburgers. Word spread and the new "hamburger stand" was in vogue. (sadly, it no longer exists)

Teatime for Brits (and Others)

Tea is properly served, created, or just sipped slowly at 10:00 a.m. and 4:00 p.m. High tea is more than tea; it is that time of day (4:00 to 6:00 p.m.) when you may serve not only tea but also dainty sandwiches, cakes, biscuits, other delicious pastries, and even fruits. Most good restaurants or hotels still use loose tea, though many have converted to tea bags. Brits often twit Americans about getting a fine cup of hot tea, then "put in lemon to sour it, sugar to sweeten it, and cream to cloud the issue!"

Theme Parks

There are four well-known parks in England, each with a different theme and location. Most can be enjoyed by adults and children. There are many, many alternative forms of amusement on the premises.

Alton Towers, Staffordshire—This vies most certainly for the longest, largest, highest thrill rides along with Cedar Point Amusement Park in Ohio.

Chessington World of Adventures, Surrey—Located south of London, with a zoo, it has themed areas including Calamity Canyon, Transylvania, and Circus World.

Legoland, Windsor—Buildings and other elements are made with forty million life-size Legos. It is a hands-on theme park with fifty amusing, interactive rides, live shows, building workshops, driving schools, and other attractions. Children can soar through the skies and ride the seas with excitement and in safety.

Thorpe Park, Surrey—This large water park features exciting rollercoasters and a very attractive and adorable pet farm.

Thetford Salutes Captain Mainwaring (Dad's Army)

Those who lived in England from 1968 to 1977 witnessed this very touching story about a group of older men who formed a platoon in the home army led by Captain Mainwaring during World War II. The TV series, *Dad's Army*, was both humorous and down-to-earth. It was so engaging that people saw the reruns in England and overseas, and some still do. It is estimated that more than eighteen million viewers watched these lads in life and their sense of military preparedness.

The Home Guard was a staple of life during the war and generally made up of older gentlemen and those who did not qualify for military service. They took their responsibilities seriously, and though never battle tested, were ready.

Some of the series was shot each summer in the Norfolk area, with the bulk of them in the lovely town of Thetford. These men became a part of TV history—and the hearts of the town's inhabitants. Even after most of the scenes had been recorded, many of the actors returned to enjoy this special town and its very caring people.

Captain Mainwaring was the leader on film and was honored by Thetford with a statue of him sitting on a park bench in full military uniform holding his swagger stick on his lap. History again is in bronze. In 2004 *Dad's Army* was voted fourth place in a BBC poll of best TV shows. In 2000 British Film Institute, voted by professionals, acclaimed *Dad's Army* as the thirteenth of one hundred best TV shows.

Trains to Bath

The Orient Express offers a very costly trip for all day, starting with a full English breakfast at the Goring Hotel in London. It is filled with sightseeing and an overnight stay. There used to be several trains each week that ran from Victoria Station and served a magnificent breakfast on board, complete with silver service, fine linens, and properly attired waiters. That has been revived from time to time but now requires an enquiry of BritRail well in advance just to see if it will be available. It's worth the effort.

Trompe L'oeil in England

One of the most glorious homes in England is Burghley House, created in the seventeenth century and featuring a multitude of fine artists from all over Europe and Britain. One of the most noted was Antonio Verrio, who spent nine years creating fabulous ceilings and the most ingenuous of wall coverings through the art of trompe l'oeil. There are six rooms, one of which gives you the instant feeling that it embodies a long hallway, festooned with window coverings, great paintings, awesome pillars, and a rich invitation to go into this new world of majestic glory and intrigue just by taking a few steps. You are almost to the wall before you realize your eyes have been tricked and there is no hallway to enter and no wonderful scenes to examine and enjoy.

There are other examples in Holkham Hall and Inveraray Castle. Even more intriguing are the titles assumed by the owner of the castle, Torquhil

Ian Campbell, the leader of that legendary Campbell clan from Scotland. He allows titles such as: the Most High, Potent, and Noble Prince; His Grace; and Duke of Argyll. Oh yes, he is also Admiral of the Western Isles, though he has never been in the navy.

Trooping the Colours

This is one of the grand customs that have occurred through the years, starting with King Charles II in the seventeenth century. The colours of a regiment were paraded in front of the troops just before battle as a rallying point. This trooping happened every day to make sure each man could identify his own regiment.

The Foot Guards also began doing this as a part of their daily Guard Mounting on Horse Guards. Current ceremonies follow that same basic line. The first known use of this salute to a sovereign's birthday happened because of the Grenadier Guards in 1748 and continued after George III ascended the throne. It was a standing order that each monarch's birthday should be noted visibly by the Trooping the Colours each year. It became an annual event, starting with King George IV, and stopped only for the two world wars.

Queen Elizabeth II has her actual birthday earlier, but the annual Trooping the Colours in London has always been, during her reign, at a time in June, chosen in advance, but usually within the first two weeks of June.

Harken to the majesty and colour of this incredible event: Since 1987 the Queen rides in a carriage. For years she rode sidesaddle and reviewed the troops, wearing the uniform of the regiment being honored. Each regiment of her personal troops, the Household Division, on Horse Guards Parade, passes by as the queen takes the salute.

This involves some 1,400 officers and men on parade, along with two hundred horses, and more than four hundred musicians from ten bands and corps of drums marching and playing as one. At least 113 words of command are given by the officer in command of the parade. The parade starts at Buckingham Palace, along the Mall to Horse Guards Palace, Whitehall, and back again. It is open to the public.

It is carefully organized and run efficiently and in a timely manner. As the clock on the Horse Guards Building strikes eleven, each troop in position, the royal procession and the queen arrives and takes the Royal Salute. The parade, as might be expected, commences with the inspection, the queen driving slowly down the ranks of all eight guards and then past the Household Cavalry. After the event, the royal family gathers on the famous balcony of Buckingham Palace to experience a Royal Air Force flypast. There are more celebrations, but you must buy tickets in advance for any or all events. It is most memorable.

Walkways and Canals

Most Brits love to walk, hike, and enjoy the outdoors. And there is plenty of it! They also know there are all kinds of places and situations, including walks through farmlands, over fences with curious high and well-maintained stiles. Then there are the woods, little babbling brooks, and great stony areas requiring some special climbing, and the little mossy knolls where you can spread out your throw, open a wicker basket, uncork the wine, and have a glorious picnic, while hearing many cheerful bird calls and the sounds of water running over rocks and even some falls.

Can you beat this? There are 15,500 miles of these combination walkways. You need a good knapsack. Maybe a wondrous wicker picnic basket from Fortnum & Mason (London—Piccadilly) plus superb wines, or a casual pickup of many good sandwiches (often as many choices as thirty to forty at Marks & Spencer (Marks & Sparks), which are in most good-sized towns and cities and can meet *all* your needs, even clothing.

Longboats and canal boats ply the wonderful locks between gorgeous waterside inns for food and rest. The boats may be rented and you may be your own helmsman, or hire someone if you so choose. You can cook on board, sleep on board, and take turns sunning on the ample decks or even enjoy life topside. Depending on where you start, there are some two to three thousand miles of canals.

SIR RICHARD N. DAVIS

Warwick Castle (the Castle of Kings) and Kenilworth

No castle in Britain, over its storied past, has ever catered to and entertained as many monarchs, queens, princes, and emperors as Warwick Castle (Warwickshire). It has withstood seiges and long battles. It has been an armory to central England. It has been firm and trusted when treachery and self-interest swirled about them but seldom in their ranks. It has stood tall since the fourteenth century. Just up the road are the old remains of a huge, once-proud castle called Kenilworth, started in 1122. This was high on a hill with a large, flowing moat surrounding the lower area, plus fortifications and ditches to impede the progress of any invaders.

This castle was a very impressive place for royalty to come to play, drink, and see the many jousts offered. There are fabulous stables for rather well-mannered steeds. Even Shakespeare, in later years, came to witness some fine offerings in some of the most elaborate theatrical pageantry of any age.

During the Civil War, parliamentary forces took Kenilworth, slowly destroyed the key walls, then drained the water defenses and let the entire castle remains slowly weaken and fall to the wiles of the elements.

The story could end there and Warwick declared the "victor" of continuity. But some twenty-two years ago, the Earl of Warwick, forty-second in line within the royal lineage to be king, sold Warwick Castle to Madame Tussaud, of wax museum fame. It is to be noted that he had a very unhappy marriage and found his long-term wife to be a rather selfish and difficult person. So he chose to divorce her. The cost was so great and the pain so difficult that he took the monies and his loyalties to a penthouse apartment in New York. Was it right to desert both his lineage and his country in the same breath?

It is fair to say that the castle truly flourishes, and Tussaud has even installed many wax figures of key persons who lived there from time to time. The armory is still impressive and totally intact. They even have all kinds of activities including archery contests, jousts, and falconry on the great lawns within the walls. Most impressive is the Kingmaker exhibition. Not to be missed is the Great Hall and state rooms.

Whitby Abbey, "The Steps," Abbess Hilda, Bede, and Captain Cook

Whitby is on the east coast of England. Its history is phenomenal. It traces back to the seventh century, with the famous abbey being created by then Abbess Hilda in 657. It was here that she became the first woman to teach monks. And her finest hour was in two parts: being part of the council that determined the dates for Easter for the Christian Church, and teaching and helping the Venerable Bede to learn how to think, write, and eventually become the father of English history. In fact, most of what is known about St. Hilda he wrote.

The abbey itself is huge, though most of it was destroyed by German warships that pummeled the coast in target practice in 1914. It is right on the coast, high up and shaped by the cold and treacherous winds from the North Sea. The abbey's housing for men was sacked by the Vikings and later rebuilt as a Benedictine abbey. The ruins from those episodes, along with the effects of the tragic shelling, are still evident.

To reach this holy place from the charming village, one must climb the 199 steps to the top. They were originally made of wood and later replaced by special stones in the seventeenth century. People still count each step to get topside.

It is also significant that Whitby became known as a port and a center for shipbuilding for ships that travel around the world. A young sailor from a nearby village, Captain James Cook, had each of his boats built there, using Whitby as his major point to replenish and repair. A statue honoring him still stands like a sentinel looking across the turbulent North Sea. There is also the famous Whalebone Arch, which looks down upon Whitby, tranquil and yet distinguished as a gentle port.

SIR RICHARD N. DAVIS

William (UK) and Willem-Alexander (Netherlands)

It is a most interesting coincidence across one sweet body of water, the English Channel. There is a prince in the Netherlands (Willem-Alexander) and another prince in Great Britain (William). Each are married and both next in line and almost sure to become a king in his own country within the next decade or so. Oh yes, *Willem* is translated from Dutch to English as "William."

William Rufus, "The Red"

Most of the monarchs of England did something good to distinguish both themselves and the royal status they had inherited. Sadly, William II was so Norman and so outlandish that he became, perhaps, the worst king ever to ascend the English throne. He also received more insults than any other monarch in England's proud history. A Victorian historian and bishop of Oxford dubbed him the "foul incarnation of selfishness in its most abhorrent form, the enemy of God and man." An eleventh-century archbishop of Canterbury called him as "dangerous as an untamed bull." The *Anglo-Saxon Chronicle* states clearly that he was "loathsome to well nigh all his people."

How did he become "William Rufus" or just "the Red"? Long strawberry blond hair, flowing over his shoulders and parted straight down the middle. And he often seemed quite red-faced, truly due in part to his ruddy complexion.

He was born in Normandy in 1056, ten years before the fateful 1066 that made his father, William the Conqueror, king of all England, and his mother, Queen Matilda. Rufus must have been smaller in height than average men. Records state him as pot-bellied and having piercing blue eyes with sparkling flecks of white that flashed whenever he was angry.

It's tough to be physically unattractive and with unpleasant personality traits. Lacking in confidence in public, he was also known to roar when very nervous. That made him appear arrogant, intimidating, and quick to take offence. Orderic Vitalis, a chronicler of the time, described him as being violent at times, when he would become "swollen with anger." His only seeming ease was with people of noble birth. He did not relate well to the commoners.

He liked the special styles of the times: shoes or boots with pointed toes curved over like a scorpion's tail. He, like others, adored long ceremonial robes with trains that cleared the earth and sleeves that were long and wide and even covered the hands. Vitalis observed: "they are almost incapable of walking or doing any kind of useful work."

The men also curled their hair with hot irons and wore feminine caps so they could be more stylish than women, "rivaling women in delicacy of person, to mince their gait walk with loose gesture."

He was vain and demanding. One day he was putting on new boots and asked a servant the cost for them. Three shillings was the response. He was irate, wishing to have ones "worth a mark of silver." The hurt servant hastened off and procured a cheaper pair and told the king they were more expensive. "These are much more suitable to royal majesty," said King William.

His father died in 1087 and left two living sons. The inheritance seemed clear. The eldest was Robert, but the old king did not like him and chose to give him an inheritance of five thousand pounds of silver but no title or power. Richard had died in his youth in a hunting accident. So William was named king.

This created envy and disharmony that prevailed in every encounter and even led to wars between both sons. These Normans, of course, had lands in both France and England. The rivalry slowed when William gave his brother Henry a ten-thousand-pound mortgage on the Duchy of Normandy. Robert was now able to go on a Crusade to the Holy Land. With William in control of all the finances, he became the ruler of Normandy while Henry was away. Those monies he handed over to Henry were not even from his own coffers.

Then he chose to assemble an army of twenty thousand soldiers, forcing every shire in England to send a particular number of men with ten shillings each to "cover expenses." Once he had ten thousand pounds, he sent the men home.

Now he could go to the Royal Treasury in Winchester (site of the first capitol of England) and seize the keys. He found sixty thousand pounds of coins and jewels and took them for his own.

Though the populace now knew of his enormous greed, they succumbed to his promises to enact fair laws and lower taxes. He did nothing! Small riots and rebellions arose, and even barons tried to overthrow him but failed. He became a bully and an oppressor. You could not even hunt on the king's lands on penalty of being hanged by your own bowstring.

He got into battles with the Scots, including stopping several invasions from up north. He killed the Scottish king, Malcolm III, at the Battle of Alnwick.

At the attack for Northumberland he faced one of the most powerful barons in all of England, Earl Robert de Mowbray. He was a successful in deposing William II who ended up dispossessed and in prison for life.

There were further rebellions, and he also suppressed invaders from Wales. He continued with castle building such as his father had done, including the fine Carlisle Castle. .

You can hardly call him a Christian, though the elegant and uplifting Durham Cathedral was erected during his reign. Match this with the incredible lands and buildings he had confiscated, including church properties, all of which were handed over to friends and others. When bishops or abbots died they were not replaced. This made churches and abbeys vulnerable to his exploitation. And it meant that much of history was written only by poor, aging monks.

It took four years to name an archbishop of Canterbury. He did reach out for an Italian Benedictine monk name Anselm. He was first summoned to aid the recovery of the king from a deep illness. The king loved the church, until he was back on his feet. Then he forgot conveniently. What irony in allowing the Cathedral to be built and then injuring the church with his constant misuse of funds and power, to the detriment of all.

He fought so much with Anselm that this saintly man went into exile, allowing the king to purloin all lands and fixtures and give them again to friends.

THOUGHTS WHILE FLYING HIGH!

When William died it created a mystery that has not yet been solved. He had a dream of his death, and a monk warned of his impending demise. Later that afternoon, hunting stags in a forest, the king was shot in the chest by an arrow and died instantly. Accident? Murder?

Just before the hunt, a blacksmith arrived with six new silver arrows. Two were given to his friend, Sir Walter Tyrell, saying: "It is only right that the sharpest should be given to the man who knows how to shoot the deadliest shots." Within hours the king was shot dead by one of those two arrows.

"Officially," Tyrell shot at a stag and it hit a tree instead and bounced off into the heart of the king. A highly accurate shooter only able to hit a tree? There was denial by Tyrell and it is said he fled back to France, even stopping to get the shoes on his horse turned around so his tracks could not be discovered or followed. Henry was present at the time and assumed the throne almost immediately. Was there some special treachery here? We can wonder, even doubt, but we will never know.

Nobody missed the king because all the men at the lodge assumed he was out hunting with friends. The body was discovered later by a woodsman. He took it in his cart to Winchester Cathedral. Out of respect for the body of the king of England, he was buried beneath the tower at the center of the cathedral.

The tower collapsed seven years later on top of the tomb, and there were those who intimated that it would have collapsed anyhow because of a weak structure. Still others thought it to be a sign of "divine judgment." The body of the king was moved to Lady's Chapel, but the original tomb of the twelfth century remains to this day in the middle of the choir stalls under the present tower. His bones lie in a mortuary chest in the cathedral.

The place where he died was marked by a Rufus Stone. It wore out and a new, iron-clad stone with inscriptions on three sides is midway between the Hampshire villages of Stoney Cross and Cadnam. A scant two hundred yards from the stone stands a pub named Sir Walter Tyrell. Just an arrow shot awry!

Thanks to Paul James, *This England,* Autumn 2010

SIR RICHARD N. DAVIS

Winchester: Capitol, Cathedral, Committed Diver

Winchester was the first capital of olde England (the second was York, and the last was, and still is, London). It was here that the noblest and finest of England's many monarchs lived and ruled: Alfred the Great. He is a story within himself (look back to the beginning of these vignettes).

The first cathedral was created in 648 but was later enlarged and now is the "new" cathedral, built in 1079. Here was another of the many examples of Benedictine monasteries that became transformed and grew into larger churches or cathedrals. The change from monastery to cathedral, in terms of building, occurred in the seventeenth century.

One of the unsung heroes of this massive edifice was William Walker. He, and others, discovered that the east end of the church was slowly being undermined by the constant flooding from the River Itchen. It was eroding the fine stone pillars at the base and they felt sure it could topple a major part of the great cathedral. It also hurt that the water table was just below the surface, forcing all work to save the building to be done underwater. For six hours each day, Mr. Walker put on his diving suit and went under water, laying sacks of cement at the base and bolstering each pillar. It worked! His diving suit is on display in the cathedral library.

In the Great Hall of Winchester, downtown, there is a huge Round Table, nailed to the wall, looking like a gigantic target with a bull's-eye in the center. This is one of many presumed relics of the Arthurian legend. It is more likely that this table was created in the thirteenth century (more than one hundred years after Arthur) by King Edward III.

There are those who would like to believe that King Arthur helped defeat the Saxons, who were still evident despite the Norman invasion and victory in 1066. He was said to have done part of this conquest near Old Sarum, the massive Neolithic fort and stronghold just two miles north of Salisbury.

It certainly has trouble fitting with the presumed location of at least one major castle in Arthur's life, Tintagel, which is on the west coast of Cornwall, high above the roiling waters of the Atlantic Ocean. He is presumed to have ruled justly and joyfully at Camelot, just north of this historic spot. It was here that the Round Table had its greatest significance, with the loyal and committed knights at table before going off to do some wondrous and mysterious deeds of valour.

Baden Hill was the site of his last great victory. He may have been wounded in that battle, for it is said he was transported to Avalon to be healed. That name is often acquainted with old Saxon comparisons to heaven.

There are those who believe that King Arthur and his queen may be buried in Glastonbury Abbey or on top of the great hill above it. There has been conjecture that the **Holy Grail** (huge chalice from the Last Supper) may also be interred there. And then there is the annual cutting from the Glastonbury Thorn, which some believe grew miraculously from the staff of Joseph of Arimathea, who once did visit England after the death of Christ.

And finally, it is to be noted that a huge hill, mountainous in stature on the east side of Edinburgh, has a great ledge and a tall rise behind it, looking as if it were a throne. It's been called "Arthur's Seat" since around the 1500s.

Wootton Bassett's Silent Tribute

A wonderful tribute went on for more than 4½ years in the sweet town of Wootton Bassett in Wiltshire because of very loving concern and English patriotism. It involved the men and women of the armed services who served abroad and made the supreme sacrifice for their country and families. The bodies of these special heroes, more than 354 personnel, were returned to Lyneham Air Base (RAF) for final preparations before being sent to the last stop with a final salute and burial.

The town started seeing so many hearses slowly driving in a procession from time to time, bearing the beloved remains of soldiers they had never met, didn't know, not even their names. Because there were some 168 military corteges that passed down the High Street, it seemed right that the mayor and council should come out to salute these boys. They did. Word grew regarding this unusual circumstance, and before long people were lining part of the route through the center of town, some waving, some with bowed heads, others crying, and many with a Union Jack in hand. It was both somber and fitting.

This solemn event grew in stature and attracted people from all over the country. It was never organized. It just happened. Some even followed this very unique procession some thirty miles northeast to the mortuary. For each new set of coffins the Union Jack was lowered to half-staff, blessed, and taken to the town's St. Bartholomew and All Saints church to be kept overnight No bell ringing for regular calls to worship. It all stopped. Two bells rang out to honor the dead.

As of 1 September 2011, Lyneham has been closed, and now the planes land at Brize Norton military airport near the mortuary outside of Oxford. The new passage will go through the village of Carterton. Hopefully, they will pick up this honored tradition.

Meanwhile, in grateful appreciation from the queen, the royal family has bestowed a new name on the town. It is now Royal Wootton Bassett.

Thanks to Janet Stobart, *Los Angeles Times*, September 1, 2011

Writers (British)

Those who converted thoughts to manuscripts, letters, and books are almost endless. And their labours and insights live on for generations to come. There are too many to receive actual mention but these are surely among the great: *William Shakespeare, Lewis Carroll, Jane Austen, Thomas Hardy, Charles Dickens, Agatha Christie, Horatio Alger, Sir Arthur Conan Doyle, Erle Stanley Gardner, J. R. R. Tolkien, C. S. Lewis, Barbara Cartland, Rhys Davies, Dick Francis, Beatrix Potter, J. K. Rowling, John Cowper Powys, Bertrand Russell, Dylan Thomas, David Jones, Robert Burns, Sir Walter Scott, Roald Dahl, Robert Louis Stevenson, Sir Philip Sydney, Edmund Spenser, Lord Alfred Tennyson*, and the list could go on for many pages. You can read about these people and their thoughts, visit their homes, and have tea with others while discussing their gifts.

THOUGHTS WHILE FLYING HIGH!

York

This is a wondrously old and special center to the three Yorkshires: North Yorkshire, West Yorkshire, and Riding. At one time, after Winchester, York became the capital city of all of olde England. That was the place, at that time, of the only archbishop other than Canterbury. And the York Minster (which has the highest number of large stained glass windows in all of England) was created and still stands as the largest (longer than four football pitches end-to-end), most noble Gothic cathedral in all of Europe.

It is one of two main cities that are strongly walled, allowing people to walk on the walls and see the city, river, and many distant vistas. The other one, Chester, is on the west coast. This one was built in AD 71, Chester in AD 79.

The significant part today is the cobbled and narrow streets winding past old and slightly new buildings. The stores keep their doors open year-round, and you can always tell, without looking, what is being offered without even going inside due to sweet or pungent or flowery aromas There are many stores with clothing, some with sweets, others with meats and fish and fowl. Still others are restaurants or offer fine china or silverware (some of which came from nearby Leeds).

The city has hosted the Romans, the Vikings, and even Constantine the Great. The Vikings claim they were never defeated, but their awful rounds of turmoil and butchery ceased when they tried to overcome York. Were they defeated by fortifications or an army? Not really! They fell in love with the fine Yorkshire ladies and decided to settle down and stay there. No more fighting!

One place you dare not miss is the Jorvik Viking Centre in Coppergate. It is extremely well done. A small "time car" takes you and your mate on a slow and wondrous trip through the "olde city," seeing active sights and cats and dogs, and smelling the many curious aromas of that time. Then you may also see some of the memorabilia still being uncovered from beneath the earth.

You also will wish to walk the short street called the "Shambles" and see many a fine old shop as it really was many, many years ago. You can even buy something there.

Don't miss the National Railway Museum (described in this book), the York Castle Museum, the Yorkshire Museum, St. Mary's Abbey, the Monk Bar, Clifford's Tower, and the Museum of Automata (history of mechanically moving objects). There also is the great candy confectioner, Rowntree Mackintosh, which gave us Kit Kat, York Mints, Yorkie bars, and Rolo. Nestlé owns part; Hershey owns another part.

Its smallest street is named Whip-Ma-Whop-Ma-Gate.   English humour!

Yorkshire Lavender

When you think of vast fields of lavender and the basis for outstanding perfumes, you must refer to the Maritime Alps in Southern France. It is also worthwhile to visit Terrington in Yorkshire, near to Malton, York, and Castle Howard. There is a farm there that has sixty acres of gorgeous and aromatic fields of exquisite lavender. And it's free!

Walk amongst the flowers, see the carefully designed plots, and sit in EJ's Licensed Tea Room or browse with delight in the shop. The key spots are the Lavender Gardens and the Specialist Plant Nursery. Try the Lavender Maze, see the Mediterranean Gardens, the Sensory Garden, the Purple Patch Garden, the Themed Gardens, Stream Garden, the Wibbly Wobbly Way, Bog Garden, Natural Wild Flower Grassland Meadow, Snakes and Ladders, the Lynne Goodwill Memorial Garden, and Sculpture Park. The sign says, "Please feel free to weed."

ABBEYS AND PRIORIES—
80 still standing in the UK

ONE OF THE MOST SIGNIFICANT PLACES TO DISCOVER IS AN **ABBEY**. MOST WERE STARTED AND BUILT BY STRONG GROUPS WITHIN THE CATHOLIC CHURCH, SUCH AS BENEDICTINES, CARTHUSIANS, CISTERCIANS, AND DOMINICANS. THEY LATER WERE TAKEN OVER BY THE CHURCH OF ENGLAND. MANY HAVE CLOSED BECAUSE THERE WERE TOO FEW NEW MONKS; OTHERS BECAUSE OF SICKNESS OR LACK OF TRAINING. THE REMAINING EDIFICES ARE INCREDIBLE. MANY ARE IN RUIN BUT CLEANED AND PREPARED FOR VISITATION. SOME WERE HUGE, LIKE THE ONE IN BURY ST. EDMUNDS IN CAMBRIDGESHIRE. THE BIGGEST MAY BE THE GORGEOUS WESTMINSTER ABBEY, SITE OF ROYAL WEDDINGS AND CORONATIONS. IT IS STILL ALIVE AND VERY ACTIVE IN LONDON. SEVERAL YEARS AGO IT WAS THOROUGHLY CLEANED ON THE OUTSIDE AFTER ALMOST A CENTURY OF GRIME AND SOOT, WHICH MADE IT LOOK RATHER GRAY, ALMOST BLACK. IT IS NOW BACK TO ITS ORIGINAL STATE. BESIDE IT LIES THE SIGNIFICANT LITTLE ST. MARGARET'S CHURCH. IT IS ALMOST A CHAPEL (IN SIZE) BESIDE THE HUGE ABBEY.

Priories are all over England and were installed for the purpose of training and housing nuns. One of the most significant ones is in Lindisfarne, which once featured both a large abbey and the beautiful priory, of which the impressive arches from the eleventh century are still visible. It is available for discovery, but you will have precious time to drive across the sands after the sea has abated. You could be caught on the Holy Island for up to five hours of you do not watch your timing. It is well worth the trip, thanks to such religious idols as St. Aidan and St. Cuthbert (buried, along with the Venerable Bede) in the towered Durham Cathedral. From early in AD 700, the Lindisfarne Gospels (almost a distant cousin of the great Book of

Kells in the library of Trinity College in Dublin, Ireland) came into being and were evacuated in AD 875 when the Vikings tried to plunder this very special place in Christian history.

BURY ST. EDMUNDS	Bury St. Edmunds, Suffolk
CERNE ABBAS	North of Dorchester, Dorset
FOUNTAINS ABBEY	Near Ripon, North Yorkshire
GLASTONBURY	Glastonbury, Somerset
HAILES	North of Winchcombe, Gloucestershire
LACOCK	Lacock, Wiltshire
LINDISFARNE	Berwick-on-Tweed, Northumberland
MELROSE	Abbey Street, Melrose, the Borders
MILTON ABBAS	Northeast of Dorchester, Dorset
RIEVAULX	Near Helmsley, North Yorkshire
WESTMINSTER	London
WHITBY	Whitby, North Yorkshire
WOBURN	Woburn, Bedfordshire

CASTLES *(among the best)—159 castles left standing*

CASTLES ARE SIGNIFICANT BECAUSE OF KINGS AND ALSO THEIR MILITARY DEFENCES. THEY WERE PRIMARY FOR THE COMMUNITIES AROUND THEM BOTH FOR PROTECTION AND FOR SUSTENANCE. THEY COULD HAVE BEEN THERE FOR A MONARCH BUT OFTEN WERE CREATED BY A BARON OR LORD OR SOME IMPORTANT DIGNITARY, AND THEY WERE HANDED DOWN TO SONS AND OTHER OFFSPRING. MANY CASTLES HAD SOME TOWNSPEOPLE LIVING INSIDE THEM. I T IS SIGNIFICANT THAT Wales has five castles that are among the very best in Britain and Europe.

ALLINGTON CASTLE	Maidstone, Kent
ARUNDEL CASTLE	Arundel, West Sussex
BALMORAL CASTLE *	Aberdeenshire, Scotland

BEAULIEU PALACE	Brockenhurst, Hampshire
BEAUMARIS CASTLE	Anglesey, North Wales
BODIAM CASTLE	Robertsbridge, East Sussex
CAERNARFON CASTLE	Menai Straits, Wales
CAERPHILLY CASTLE	North of Cardiff, Wales
CAISTER CASTLE	Great Yarmouth, Norfolk
CASTLE HOWARD	North of York (City), North Yorkshire
CONWY CASTLE	Aberconwy & Colwyn, North Wales
EDINBURGH CASTLE	Edinburgh, Scotland
FLINT CASTLE	Flintshire, North East Wales
GLAMIS CASTLE *	Angus, Scotland
HARLECH CASTLE	Gwynedd, North Wales
HEVER CASTLE	Near Edenbridge, Kent
LEEDS CASTLE	Southeast of Maidstone, Kent
PONTEFRACT CASTLE	Wakefield, W Y
RAGLAN CASTLE	Gwent, South Wales
STIRLING CASTLE	Stirling, Scotland
TINTAGEL CASTLE	West coast, Cornwall
TOWER OF LONDON	London
WARWICK CASTLE	Warwick, Warwickshire
WINDSOR CASTLE *	Windsor, Berkshire

*Royal Residences

CATHEDRALS *(a few of the fine ones)*— *(grand total of 56 in the UK)*

MOST CATHEDRALS WERE ERECTED TO BENEFIT THE PARISH OR THE DIOCESE (CHURCH OF ENGLAND) FOR A RESIDENT BISHOP LIVING WITHIN THAT SEE. MANY TOOK AT LEAST ONE HUNDRED YEARS TO BUILD, SOME LESS TIME. THERE ARE THOSE FEW THAT WERE FOREVER BEING FINISHED. MANY WERE DESTROYED BY DECAY OR ACTS OF NATURE AND SOME BY BOMBS AND SHELLING. IN MANY

CASES, SUCH AS COVENTRY, A NEW CATHEDRAL ROSE NEAR TO THE OLD. TODAY THEY ARE PRESERVED VERY CAREFULLY AND AT GREAT COST TO ALL WHO CARE ABOUT THEM. THAT IS WHY VOLUNTARY DONATIONS OFTEN ARE REQUESTED OR TICKETS MAY BE PURCHASED TO HELP SUSTAIN THEIR BEAUTY AND VALUE TO COMMUNITY AND THE WORLD.

BRISTOL	Bristol, Somerset
CANTERBURY	Canterbury, Kent
COVENTRY	Coventry, West Midlands
DURHAM	Durham, County Durham
ELY	Ely, Cambridgeshire
EXETER	Exeter, Devonshire
GLOUCESTER	Gloucester, Gloucestershire
LINCOLN	Lincoln, Lincolnshire
LLANDAFF	Cardiff, Wales
NORWICH	Norwich, Norfolk
PETERBOROUGH	Peterborough, Cambridgeshire
RIPON	Ripon, North Yorkshire
SALISBURY	Salisbury, Wiltshire
ST. PAUL'S	London
WELLS	Wells, Somerset
WINCHESTER	Winchester, Hampshire
YORK MINSTER	York, North Yorkshire

FLOWER SHOWS

THESE TWO SHOWS ARE AMONG THE BEST AND LARGEST IN THE WORLD. THEY ARE OPEN FOR SEVERAL KEY DAYS AND DESERVE A LOOK ON THE INTERNET AND PERHAPS EVEN A RESERVATION (BOOKING) TO VISIT.

CHELSEA FLOWER SHOW	Royal Hospital, Chelsea (mid-May)
HARROGATE FLOWER SHOWS	North Yorkshire (April and September)

SIR RICHARD N. DAVIS

GARDENS

ONE WAG ONCE SAID, "A MAN IS NOT AN ENGLISHMAN IF HE DOES NOT HAVE A GARDEN." MOST PEOPLE DO HAVE EVEN A MODEST PLOT; A LARGE AND SELECT GROUP HAVE ELABORATE AND WELL-MAINTAINED GARDENS THAT ARE BREATHTAKING TO VISIT. SOME OF THE GREATEST LANDSCAPE GARDENERS OF BRITAIN ARE MENTIONED IN THIS BOOK. THERE IS A TARIFF TO VISIT THE LARGER AND BETTER-TENDED GARDENS IN THE UK. IT IS A WORTHY COST TO ENJOY BOTH SIGHT AND AROMA.

BODIAM CASTLE	Robertsbridge, East Sussex
BODNANT GARDEN	Near Conwy, North Wales
CHILHAM CASTLE	West of Canterbury
HADDON HALL	Bakewell, Derbyshire
HADDONSTONE SHOW GARDENS	East Haddon, Northampton
HIDCOTE MANOR	Hidcote, Bartrim
KEW PALACE	Richmond (south of London)
NYMAN GARDENS	West Sussex
POWIS CASTLE	Welshpool, Powis, Wales
SISSINGHURST CASTLE GARDEN	South of Leeds Castle, Kent
SNOWSHILL MANOR	Snowshill, the Cotswolds
STOURHEAD	Stourton, Wiltshire
STOWE LANDSCAPE GARDENS	Buckinghamshire
STUDLEY ROYAL WATER GARDEN	North of Ripon, North Yorkshire
TRELISSICK GARDEN	Feock or Truro, Cornwall
WISLEY GARDEN	Woking

MANOR HOMES—*136 in England*

IT'S A TRUISM THAT MOST MANORS WERE ESTABLISHED BY MEN OF PEERAGE AND WEALTH, OFTEN BEING THE CENTER OF

A COMMUNITY THAT BOTH HONORED THE LORD AND SERVED HIM AS A WAY OF LIFE. MANY OF THESE LORDS BECAME A NATURAL PART OF THE HOUSE OF LORDS (THAT STILL OBTAINS TODAY). SOME WERE GREAT MANAGERS AND BENEVOLENT BOTH TO THOSE WHOM THEY SERVED AND OTHERS WHO VISITED SOME OF THESE GLORIOUS ESTATES. STILL OTHERS WERE VINDICTIVE, HARSH, AND GAVE LITTLE TO TOWN NEEDS. GREED AND SELFISHNESS WERE OFTEN IN THE MINORITY.

CASTLE COMBE	Combe, Wiltshire
HATFIELD HOUSE	Hatfield, Herefordshire
HEVER CASTLE	Hever, Kent
HUGHENDEN MANOR	High Wycombe, Buckinghamshire
IGHTHAM MOTE	Seven Oaks, Kent
KNOLE HOUSE	Knole, Kent
NUNNINGTON HALL	Nunnington, North Yorkshire
STOKESAY CASTLE	Stokesay, Shropshire
SUTTON COURT	Stowey, Somerset
WADDESDON MANOR	Waddesdon, Buckinghamshire

MUSEUMS (LONDON)—more than 240 in London alone

BRITAIN HAS LONG BEEN KNOWN FOR THE ENORMOUS TREASURES THAT WERE BOUGHT AND DISPLAYED WITHIN THE CONFINES OF THE HOMES OF NOBLES AND ARISTOCRATS, MOST OF THEM RATHER WEALTHY. IN THE LATE 1970S, THERE WERE HEAVY TAXES LEVIED ON THE LANDOWNERS, ESPECIALLY THOSE WITH PRIZED POSSESSIONS. BECAUSE OF THIS, MANY FINE PAINTINGS, SCULPTURE, AND OTHERS WORKS OF ART WERE SOLD TO FOREIGN INTERESTS IN ONE OF THE LARGEST CULTURAL DRAINS ANY COUNTRY EVER ENDURED.

TWO GOOD THINGS BEGAN TO HAPPEN: MUSEUMS BOUGHT UP AS MUCH AS THEY COULD AFFORD. THE NATIONAL

TRUST WAS NOW BECOMING HIGHLY IMPORTANT TO ALL OF THE UK AS A MEANS OF PRESERVING AND SAVING ALL KINDS OF ART THROUGH THIS CULTURAL ORGANIZATION THAT NOW OWNS OR MANAGES WELL OVER SIX HUNDRED KEY BUILDINGS, HOMES, OR OTHER EDIFICES.

THE MUSEUMS OF LONDON CAN VIE WITH MANY OF THE GREAT MUSEUMS OF THE WORLD FOR ART AND CULTURAL OBJECTS. THERE ARE ALSO GREAT PLACES FOR NATURAL HISTORY, ASTONOMY, SCIENCE, MILITARY, AND THE MULTIFACETED VICTORIA AND ALBERT MUSEUM WITH ITS AWESOME DIVERSITY OF ARTIFACTS, AS WELL AS APPLIED ARTS AND PHOTOGRAPHY. ONE CAN ALSO MARVEL AT THE NATIONAL RAILWAY MUSEUM IN YORK (LARGEST ANYWHERE) AND THE REDOUBTABLE TOUCH OF OLD MINING AND TRAINS AT THE OPEN-AIR MUSEUM (THE BEAMISH COUNTY DURHAM).

BRITISH MUSEUM	Great Russell Street WC1
COURTAULD GALLERY & SOMERSET HOUSE	The Strand WC2
DULWICH PORTRAIT GALLERY	College Road SE21
IMPERIAL WAR MUSEUM	Lambeth Road SE1
NATURAL HISTORY	Cromwell Road SW7
NATIONAL GALLERY	Trafalgar Square WC2
NATIONAL PORTRAIT GALLERY	St. Martins Place WC2
TATE GALLERY	Milbank SW1
TATE MODERN	25 Sumner Street (Bankside) SE1 9TG
VICTORIA AND ALBERT	Cromwell Road SW7
WALLACE COLLECTION	Manchester Square W1

NATIONAL RAILWAY MUSEUM

It has taken over 80 years to build both the museum in York and several other fine outlets around England to show the many different locomotives and carriages, not to mention old stations and their wonderful equipment. Its in three huge halls and covers over 20 acres.

Without any doubt the most popular parts of this enormous Main Museum center in great locomotives and other parts of special trains. There are over 100 locomotives and 200+ items of real rolling stock. Most built here and used here. This is the largest museum of its type in Great Britain. If you are in York it is a brief walk from the railway station.

Among the most attractive and best known are the *Mallard*, the *Flying Scotsman* (described in the Vignettes), *BoBo No. 1, Stirling Single, Deltic, Eagle* (first class kitchen car), *Class 37, APT-P* (electric power car), *Evening Star*, and the two grand "oldies" of the early years of railroading: *PuffingBilly* (1813-1814) and *Stephenson's Rocket* (1829) George Stephenson is generally credited as the maker of both the earliest and the finest locomotives ever built.

There were numerous Royal Trains built in gaudy array for Kings, Queens and at least three Duchess members of the British trains and carriages. The most modern was known as the *Duchess of Hamilton*. The others were *Duchess of Windsor* and *Duchess of York*.

For Sheer opulence, comfort and regal adornment you will love these five beauties:

Queen Adelaides Saloon (oldest preserved carriage in Europe)
Queen Victoria's "Palace on Wheels", most famous and popular of all
King Edward VII's royal carriage (1902 – used heavily in Scotland).
Royal Saloon (built for King George VI and the Queen mother – WWII)
Built for maximum protection for royal riders
Black Five (1935 – stands at head of the royal collection)

PARKS *(LONDON)*

EACH PARK IN LONDON IS THERE FOR A REASON. THERE ARE MANY SMALLER PARKS AROUND THE LONDON AREA. BEST-KNOWN ONES CONTAIN PALACES, ONE HAS THE

LARGEST GARDEN IN LONDON, ANOTHER IS GREEN BECAUSE THE QUEEN ORDERED ALL THE FLOWERS REMOVED AFTER SHE FOLLOWED THE KING MANY YEARS AGO, SEEING HIM PULLING UP POSIES TO ATTRACT ONE OF THE COURTESANS OF THEIR COURT. ANOTHER IS NOTED FOR ITS ORATORS ON A SUNDAY, AND ANOTHER PARK WITH A POND WITH TINY BOAT RACES AND SAILING. YOU ALSO CAN STRETCH OUTAND REST IN EACH PARK.

BATTERSEA	London SW11 4NJ
GREEN	Piccadilly Road SW1
HAMPSTEAD HEALTH	Spaniards Road NW3
HOLLAND	230 Kensington High Street W8
HYDE	Bayswater Road W8
KENSINGTON GARDENS	Kensington High Street W8
KEW GARDENS	Richmond SW15
REGENT'S	Marylebone Road NW1 4NR
RICHMOND	King's Road TW10 5HS
ST. JAMES	Horse Guards Road SW1A 2BJ

PERFORMING ARTS
(LONDON AND THE UK)

ENGLAND HAS LONG BEEN KNOWN FOR ITS DRAMATISTS, MUSICIANS, POETS AND AUTHORS, DANCERS, AND BANDS AND ORCHESTRAS. YOU CAN FIND TRUE VENUES FOR EACH OF THESE GREAT PRESENTATIONS AND OTHERS IN LONDON. THESE ARE LISTINGS TO HELP YOU KNOW WHAT TO LOOK FOR. CONSULT THE LOCAL NEWSPAPERS (LISTED ELSEWHERE), RADIO OR TELEVISION, AND THE INCREDIBLE **VISIT BRITAIN**, THE VOICE OF ALL ENGLAND AND ITS MANY, MANY HAPPENINGS. THEIR INFORMATION IS DRAMATIC, IS USEFUL, AND FREE:

THOUGHTS WHILE FLYING HIGH!

Visit Britain
1 Palace Street
London SW1E 5HX
Website: www.visitbritain.com

BALLET:

Royal Ballet
Ballet Rambert
Festival Ballet
New London Ballet
London Contemporary Dance Theatre
Scottish Ballet
Sadler's Wells
ICA
The Royalty Theatre
Chisenhale Dance Space

FESTIVALS:

Edinburgh Festival
Three Choirs Festival
Glyndebourne Summer Opera
City of London Festival
F&M Jazz Festival
UK Music Festival
London Jazz Festival
Design Festival
Bridge Festival
Strawberry Festiva
Festival of Wild Flowers & Music in Church
Exhibition of Village Activities in Hall

SIR RICHARD N. DAVIS

MUSIC:

English Chamber Orchestra
Academy of St. Martin-in-the-Fields
London Jazz
London Symphony Orchestra
London Banqueting Ensembles

OPERA:

Royal Opera House
English National Opera
English National Opera North
Welsh National Opera
Scottish National Opera

VENUES FOR BALLET, JAZZ, OPERA, POP, ROCK, THEATRE:

Royal Albert Hall	Kensington Gore SW7
Wigmore Hall	Wigmore St. W1
Royal Opera House	Floral St. WC2
London Coliseum	St. Martin's Lane WC2
The Place Theatre	17 Duke's Rd. SE1
The Barbican	Silk St. EC2
Southbank Centre	Belvedere Rd. SE1
Wembley Stadium and Arena	Empire Way, Wembley
Brixton Academy	211 Stockwell Rd. SW9
The Forum	9-17 Highgate Rd. NW5
Hippodrome	Leicester Square WC2

Limelight	136 Shaftsbury Ave. W1
Wag Club	35 Wardour St. W1
Ministry of Sound	103 Gaunt St. SE1
Madame Jojo's	8-10 Brewer St. W1
Heaven	Villiers St. WC2 (under Arches)
Le Scandale	53-54 Berwick St. W1
Gossips	69 Dean St. W1
Fridge	Town Hall Parade, Brixton
Stringfellows	16-19 Upper St. Martin's

THEATRES (LONDON)—104 of all kinds

The earliest plays seem to have occurred in the Middle Ages, often centering in Mystery Plays, which depicted events from the Bible and even some saints. There were Miracle Plays THAT devoted lots of writing and presentation to the actual miracles of the Holy Bible.

Modern theatres turn mostly on the brilliance of thought and acting occasioned by the works of Shakespeare. Certainly there were others who also began writing in those days, such as Marlowe. Women were not allowed to act in these plays. Female parts were often played by young lads whose voices had not yet changed.

One of the oldest theatres was the Globe, created in the time of Shakepeare in 1599. It later burned to ground, was rebuilt, and then closed in 1642. In 1997 the new Globe was built in Southwark and has been open and visited daily by London visitors.

ADELPHI	Earlham St. WC2 9AU
ALDWYCH	Aldwych WC2
APOLLO	17 Wilton Rd. SWIV 1LL
CAMBRIDGE	Earlham St. WC2
GARRICK	Charing Cross Rd. WC2H 0HH
GIELGUD	Shaftsbury Ave. W1
GLOBE	21 New Globe Walk SE1 8DT
HER MAJESTY'S	Haymarket SW1

LONDON PALLADIUM	Argyll St. W1
LYRIC	Shaftsbury Ave. W1D 7ESNEW
LONDON	Drury Lane WC2B 5PW
PALACE	Shaftsbury Ave. W1D 8H1
PHOENIX	Charing Cross Rd. WC2H OJP
PICCADILLY	Denman St. W1D 7DY
PRINCE EDWARD	Old Compton St. W1D 4HS
PRINCE OF WALES	Coventry St. W1
QUEENS	Shaftsbury Ave. W1D 6BA
SAVOY	Strand WC2R OEU
SHAFTSBURY	210 Shaftsbury Ave. WC2H
THEATRE ROYAL	Haymarket W1
VAUDEVILLE	Strand WC2
WYNDHAM'S	Charing Cross Rd. WC2H 0DA

Half-price same-day tickets can be obtained before 11:00 a.m. at Leicester Square.

PUBS *(LONDON)*—*7,000 in London*

Something needs to be said about The Pub. It is definitely a British institution. For many centuries it was open only to men. Women were finally allowed to enter if accompanied by a gentleman. That right is within the last one hundred years—in many cases, even more recent. Now it is open to families in most pubs. There are special times to be open and precise times to close.

Pubs is the shortened form of *publick Houses*. Many had their own breweries on site and generally specialized in making ales. Today you can have a pint of whatever you wish (there is also the legendary "Yard of Ale" made of glass and filled to the brim). The challenge is to lift it and drink all of it (chugalug) without stopping. Rare is the man who can do that. And there is the prime set of pumps in each location so several different kinds of ale or beer can be drawn. This is called a "draught" (pronounced "draft"). There are also bottled ales and beers, some of them from other parts of the world.

FOOD IS ALSO SERVED IN SOME PUBS. FOR SNACK-TYPE OFFERINGS, ask for "pub grub." Those that have restaurants have specific menus and specific times they are open (generally for TWO TO THREE HOURS IN THE EVENING).

The signs, always hanging high and very noticeable, are sweet invitations with delightful names and even some quaint pictures or caricatures, all painted. The name most often used is "the Red Lion."

There is hardly a village, town, or city without at least one pub. More often there are many, some with distinctive histories and well-known appeals. The oldest pub, according to Guinness World Records, Is Ye Olde Fighting Cocks in St. Albans, created AD 795.

It is fairly easy to find and buy signs, mugs, and other paraphernalia.

ANCHOR & HOPE	Waterloo, Greater London
ANGEL**	101 Bermondsey Wall SE16
BLACK FRIAR	174 Queen Victoria St. EC4
CHANDOS	29 St. Martin's Lane WC2
CITTIE OF YORKE	22 High Holborn WC1
COACH & HORSES	Soho
DIRTY DICKS	202 Bishopgate EC2M 4NR
DOVE	19 Upper Mall, Hammersmith W6
GEORGE INN **	77 Borough High St. SE1
HOOPS & GRAPES****	47 Aldgate High St. EC3
LAMB & FLAG *	33 Rose St. WC2
NARROW	Limehouse, Greater London
OLDE BELL ****	95 Fleet St. EC4
PARADISE BY WAY OF KENSAL GREEN	Kilburn Lane
PROSPECT OF WHITBY ***	57 Wapping Wall, Wapping
RED LION	2 Duke of York St. SW1
SCARSDALE ARMS	21 Edwardes Square W8
SPANIARDS INN *****	Spaniards Rd. NW3
STAR	Belgravia Mews SW1
WHITE HART **	191 Drury Lane WC2
WHITE HORSE	Parsons Green
YE OLDE CHESHIRE CHEESE	145 Fleet St. EC4
YE OLDE WATLING ****	29 Watling St. EC4

* Oldest pub in London

** Among the oldest pubs
*** Most famous pub in London
**** Survivors of the Great Fire
***** Most myth-saturated pub

PUBS (UK)—more than 60,000

DEVONSHIRE HOUSE	126 Devonshire Road, Chiswick W4
FLEECE	The Cross, Bretforton
GEORGE HOTEL (oldest in UK)	High Street, Stamford
FALKLAND ARMS	Great Tew, Oxfordshire
FEATHERS	High Street, Ledbury, Herefordshire
OLD NAGS HEAD	Edale, Hope Valley, Derbyshire S33
RHYDSPENCE	Whitney-on-Wye, Herefordshire
T.G.I. FRIDAY'S BAR	Manchester
TIPPERARY INN PUB	Meer End, Kenilworth, Warwickshire
WILD DUCK	Ewen, Drakes Island, Cirencester
WOODFALLS INN	The Ridge, Woodfalls, Salisbury
YE OLDE TRIP TO JERUSALEM	Castle Road, Nottingham

PUBLIC SCHOOLS (Called Private Schools in the United States)—2,500 public schools in UK

BRADFIELD
CLIFTON
DULWICH
ETON
HARROW
MALVERN
MARLBOROUGH
RUGBY

THOUGHTS WHILE FLYING HIGH!

WELLINGTON
WINCHESTER

ROYAL RESIDENCES AND PALACES

As one can see, there are quite a few, and nearly all of the Royal Residences have times for visitation during the year. The Other palaces are not owned by the Crown but are there for reasons that go way back in history. They represent a special time in both English and Scottish history. Perhaps the most notable of the places is the birth site of Winston Churchill (Blenheim in Woodstock, Oxfordshire).

BALMORAL CASTLE *	Royal Deeside, Scotland
BEAULIEU PALACE	Brockenhurst, Hampshire
BLENHEIM PALACE	Woodstock, Oxon
BUCKINGHAM PALACE *	London
CLARENCE HOUSE *	London
DUNFERMLINE PALACE	Fife, Scotland
FALKLAND PALACE *	Fife, Scotland
HAMPTON COURT PALACE	East Molesey, Surrey
HOLYROODHOUSE PALACE *	Edinburgh, Scotland
KENSINGTON PALACE *	Knightsbridge, London
PALACE OF ST. JAMES *	Marlborough Road, London
SCONE	Northeast of Perth, Scotlamd
SANDRINGHAM HOUSE *	North Norfolk
WINDSOR CASTLE *	Windsor, Berkshir*Royal Residences

STATELY HOMES—*hundreds in England, Scotland, and Wales*

These are among the country's finest treasures. They were owned by families for generations, accumulating and passing on great art, antiques, sculpture, and other special holdings.

ALTHORP (Lady Diana's home)   Althorp, Northamptonshire
APSLEY HOUSE   London
ATHELHAMPTON HOUSE   Dorchester, Dorset
AUDLEY END HOUSE   Saffron Walden Essex
  AND GARDENS
BLICKLING HALL   Blickling, Norfolk
BURGHLEY HOUSE   Stamford, Lincolnshire
BUSCOT PARK   Faringdon, Oxfordshire
CHARTWELL HOUSE   Westerham, Kent
CHATSWORTH HOUSE   Chesterfield, Derbyshire
HARDWICK HALL   Chesterfield, Derbyshire
HAREWOOD HOUSE   North of Leeds, North Yorkshire
HATFIELD HOUSE   Hertfordshire
HOLKHAM HALL   West of Wells-by-thSea, Norfolk
HOPETOUN HOUSE   West Lothian, Scotland
KEDLESTON HALL   Derby, Derbyshire
KNEBWORTH HOUSE   Knebworth, Hertfordshire
KNOLE   Sevenoaks, Kent
LONGLEAT HOUSE   Warminster, Wiltshire
OTLEY HALL   Otley, Suffolk
RAGLEY HALL   Alcester, Warwickshire
ROYAL PAVILION   Old Steine, Brighton
STOURHEAD HOUSE   Stourton, Wiltshire
SYON HOUSE   London Road, Brentford
UPTON HOUSE   Banbury, Warwickshire
WADDESDON MANOR   Northwest of Aylesbury, Oxon
WILTON HOUSE   Wilton, Wiltshire

TRADITIONAL ENGLISH FOODS (a sampling)

CORNISH PASTIE (meat, potatoes, veggies, wee dessert, folded-over pastry shell)
COTTAGE PIE (minced beef)

CUMBERLAND SAUSAGE (best known but one of many by region)
DOVER SOLE (flat fish, served grilled on the bone, firm texture, delicate flavor)
FISH AND CHIPS (cod or haddock or skate or plaice, with chips [Fries]
PLOUGHMAN'S LUNCH (slice/hunk of cheese, crusty bread, onion, garnish, beer)
ROAST BEEF AND YORKSHIRE PUDDING (batter, like a popover) and beef with gravy, potatoes, and veggies)
SHEPHERD'S PIE (minced lamb)
STEAK AND KIDNEY PIE (chunks of beef and kidney with thick gravy in pastry crust)

At one time some favorite American fast-food restaurants were in evidence. Years ago the number one in Britain and England was Kentucky Fried Chicken; in certain parts of England and Europe McDonald's was the favorite. In recent years the best-selling American pizza was Pizza Hut. Others are there as well.

UNIVERSITIES AND SCHOOLS
280 in England, Scotland, and Wales

OXFORD   Eleventh century—thirty-eight colleges
CAMBRIDGE   1209 —thirty-one colleges
ST. ANDREWS, Scotland 1413
EDINBURGH, Scotland   1583
LONDON SCHOOL OF ECONOMICS   1895
IMPERIAL COLLEGE (London)   1913
BATH
BRISTOL
DURHAM
EXETER
LANCASTER
LEEDS
MANCHESTER
WARWICK
YORK

SIR RICHARD N. DAVIS

VILLAGES OF ENGLAND *(small, but quite English and lovely)*

This is the very heart of English history. These are the places with quaint names and special traditions. They are often quite small and not always easy to find. They are seldom included in large tours that seek to show the big cities and the noted treasures of easily found places. The small village often contains many of the wondrous and timeless looks, attitudes, and scenery of the past.

NORTHERN COUNTIES:
Bamburgh—Northumberland
Chipping—Lancashire
Gainford—Durham
Hawkshead—Cumbria
Heptonstall—West Yorkshire
Linton-in-Craven—North Yorkshire
Prestbury—Cheshire

MIDLAND COUNTIES:
Abbots Bromley—Staffordshire
Acton Burnell—Shropshire
Chaddesley Corbett—Worcestershire
Cottesbrooke—Northamptonshire
Dorchester—Oxfordshire
Edensor—Derbyshire
Hallaton—Leicestershire
Southwell—Nottinghamshire
Welford-on-Avon—Warwickshire
Wembley—Herefordshire

EASTERN COUNTIES:
Castle Bytham—Lincolnshire
Dedham—Essex
Hemingford Grey—Cambridgeshire
Heydon—Norfolk
Lavenham—Suffolk

SOUTHERN COUNTIES:
Aldbury—Hertfordshire
Amberley—Sussex

Elham—Kent
Elstow—Bedfordshire
Eton—Berkshire
Nether Winchendon—Buckinghamshire
Ockley—Surrey
Wherwell—Hampshire
WESTERN COUNTIES:
Cerne Abbas—Dorset
Clovelly—Devon
Dunster—Somerset
Lacock—Wiltshire
Lower and Upper Slaughter—Gloucestershire
Mevagissey—Cornwall

SPECIALTY STORES, SHOPS ETC
(London Area)

BERMONDSEY	Bermondsey Square SE1
BRICK LANE MARKET	Brick Lane E1
BURBERRY	18-22 Haymarket SW1
CAMDEN LOCK MARKET	Chalk Farm Rd. NW1
COVENT GARDEN	The Piazza WC2
FORTNUM & MASON	Piccadilly Rd. W1
GIEVES & HAWKES	1 Savile Row W1
GREENWICH MARKET	Approach SE10
HARRODS	87-135 Brompton Rd. SW1
JASPER CONRAN	6 Burnsall St. SW3
JOHN LOBB	9 St. James St. SW1
KATHARINE HAMNETT	20 Sloane St. SW1
LAURA ASHLEY	256-258 Regent St. W1
LIBERTY	210-220 Regent St. W1
MARKS & SPENCER	173 & 458 Oxford St. W1
PORTOBELLO ROAD MARKET	Portobello Rd. W10

SELFRIDGES	400 Oxford St. W1
VIVIENNE WESTWOOD	6 Davies St. W1

SUPERMARKETS
(the largest that are all over the land)

ASDA
COOP
MORRISONS
SAINSBURY'S
TESCO
WAITROSE

TEA ROOMS *(some also sell tea and implements for making tea)*

You are not truly British unless you have a kettle and are ready to "put it on" whenever guests or family arrive. It is quite proper at 10:00 A.M. or 4:00 P.M. or even High Tea between 6:00 and 9:00 P.M. High Tea generally includes biscuits, cakes, and special sweets.

There is a culinary art to this most fashionable of English Traditions. But it is not the fashions or manners that count the most: it's the TEA.

Most tea lovers trace the beginnings (in Britain) to the 1600s and the first teas sent from China. It was more than fashionable. It did give hopes of treating scurvy, colds, and other infections.

Over the years it was part of the entertaining amongst the elite and most privileged, especially afternoon tea. It became even more appealing as fine china, special serviettes, and strainers came into vogue. It was rare that people did not have the leaves of several types of tea on hand at all times. There were even stores with large bins of teas, creating an aroma and offering a sure look at the best and freshest of current available tea leaves.

Nowadays, many hotels, restaurants, and even homemakers have resorted to the use of tea bags. True tea lovers will argue that this was not only unconventional but also crude, because often you get the "clippings" from leaves and not the full-bodied leaf at its best, carefully nurtured in a proper teapot.

Whatever your choice, there are many, many places to have a very quiet cup, a reassuring cup, a love cup, or a traditional 4:00 P.M. touch of class, including biscuits, scones, and finer sandwiches. Here are some places in LONDON to indulge these sensory moments of British teas.

BROWN'S HOTEL	22-24 Dover St. W1
CLARIDGE'S HOTEL	Brook St. W1A 2JQ
DORCHESTER HOTEL	53 Park Lane W1A 2HJ
FORTNUM & MASON	Piccadilly W1
GORING HOTEL	Boston Place SW1
GROSVENOR HOUSE HOTEL	Park Lane W1
HARRODS	87-135 Brompton Rd. SW1
HYATT REGENCY—THE CHURCHILL	Portman Square W1H 7BH
LANDMARK	222 Marylebone Rd. NW1 6JQ
LANGHAM	1c Portland Place, Regent St., W1B 1JA
MANDARIN ORIENTAL	Hyde Park
MILESTONE	1 Kensington Court W8 5DL
ORANGERY	Kensington Palace SW1
RITZ PALM COURT	Piccadilly W1V 9DG
SAVOY HOTEL	The Strand WC2R OEU

TEAROOMS *(elsewhere in the UK)*

BETTY'S	1 Parliament Street, Harrogate (Plus York, Ilkley, and Northallerton)
BLACK SWAN HOTEL	Helmsley, North Yorkshire

BRIDGE TEA ROOM	24a Bridge St. Bradford-on-Avon
CAVENDISH HOTEL	Garden Room, Baslow, Derbyshire
CAKE TABLE TEA ROOM	Fishmarket St. Thaxted, Sussex
DARTMOOR TEAROOMS	3 Cross St., Moretonhampstead, Devon
LADY NORTHWICK'S TEA ROOM	The Post Office Square, Blockley
LORD OF THE MANOR HOTEL	Upper Slaughter, Gloucestershire
NARE HOTEL	**Veryan-in-Roseland, Cornwall TR2 5PF**
OLD FIRE ENGINE HOUSE	25 St Mary's Street – Ely, Camb
PEACOCKS TEAROOM	65 Waterside – Ely, Camb CB7 4AU
PUMP ROOM	Stall Street, Bath BA1 11.Z
SALLY LUNN'S HOUSE	4 North. Parade Passage, Bath. Avon
SHEPHERD'S TEA ROOMS	35 Little London, Chichester
THE RECTORY	Bude, Cornwall EX23 9SR
VIOLET'S AND CRÈME	28 Market Place, Henley-on-Thames
ROCKE COTTAGE TEAROOMS	Clungunford, Wales SY7 OFX
E. BOTHARD & SONS, LTD	35139 Skinner St., Whitby, YOZ1 3RH
ANGEL HOTEL	High St. Llandloes, Powys SY18 6BY
THE BALMORAL HOTEL	1 Princes St, Edinburgh, Scotland EH2 2EQ
MIMI'S BAKEHOUSE	63 The Shore, Edinburgh, Scotland EH6 6RA
WILLOW TEA ROOMS	21 Sauchiehall St., Glasgow, Scotland G2 3EX
KILRAVOCK CASTLE	Scotland, between Croy & Clephanton IV2, 7-10 miles NE of Inverness

THEME PARKS AND AN OPEN-AIR MUSEUM

There is an honest temptation to believe that only in America can you find outstanding parks or places with grand and swooping rides and high-speed roller coasters. There are those with themes as well. It is also true in Britain and at very fine parks that will surprise one with its multiple choices and outstanding delights such as cotton candy, special ices, and even corn sticks. The height and speed of rides may often challenge the best in many other places.

The open-air museum is an entirely different entity because it is a salute and reminder of the great days of coal mining and building grand cars and locomotives that ended up being sent many times to both America and other foreign lands. You can even enter a part of the mine, ride on the old-fashioned trolley around the some three hundred acres, and learn about the incredible inventiveness and foresight of one George Stephenson, considered by many to be the father of the best steam engines of the nineteenth century. He even designed railways that were considered impossible to create. This is a place to be in touch with a bit of this monumental history. (see York and the largest railway museum in the world: The National Railway Museum.)

Legoland is also unique for the entire park and buildings are created with LEGOS (giant-sized when compared to children's sets). IT's Great fun for children, and parents marvel at the ingenuity of the Lego.

ALTON TOWERS	Alton, Staffordshire
BEAMISH MUSEUM	(open air), Stanley, County Durham
CAMELOT THEME PARK	Chorley, Lancashire
CHESSINGTON WORLD OF ADVENTURES	Chessington, Surrey
LEGOLAND	Windsor, Berkshire
NATIONAL RAILWAY MUSEUM	York, North Yorkshire
PLEASURE BEACH THEME PARK	Blackpool
THORPE PARK	Chertsey, Surrey

TRANSPORTATION

Tubes, Underground, "Subway"	Tickets for one ride, returns, two-plus days
National Express Coaches	Discounted lines all over the UK
National Rail	For all of Britain (BritRail)
Chunnel	Chunnel to France (Folkestone to Calais)

Original London Sightseeing Tour *

* "Hop on" for a twenty-four-hour pass. Start at Trafalgar Square, Piccadilly Circus, Embankment Station, Victoria, Grosvenor Gardens, or the Marble Arch.

London highlights: fourteen places to see, hear about, get off, get back on, and go to other venues.

Includes free hop-on, hop-off
Thames River cruise
Three free walking tours.
Included also are Changing of the Guard walk and Classic walk.

Departs every fifteen to twenty minutes.

MAINLINE RAIL STATIONS (primary)

Station Location	Services	Natl Service	
Charing Cross	Westminster	SE	Kent, Sussex
Euston	Camden	NW	Watford DC Line
Liverpool			
Manchester			
King's Cross	Camden	N	East Coast chief
Cambridge			
Liverpool	London City	E, NE	Great Eastern
Main Line			

THOUGHTS WHILE FLYING HIGH!

East of England			
Stansted Airport			
Marylebone	Westminster	NW	Buckinghamshire
Oxfordshire			
Warwickshire			
Birmingham			
Paddington	Westminster	W	Great Western
Main Line			
Heathrow Airport			
St. Pancras	Camden	N, NW, S, SE	Gatwick Airport
Luton Airport			
Midland Main			
Victoria	Westminster	S, SE, SW	Kent, Sussex
Gatwick Airport			
Waterloo	Lambeth	SW	Surrey, Hampshire
South West			

NEWSPAPERS (LONDON)—a few

Daily Express and Sunday Express
Daily Mail and Mail on Sunday
Daily Star
Daily Telegraph and Sunday Telegraph
Evening Standard
Financial Times
Guardian
Independent and Independent on Sunday
Mirror
Observer on Sunday
Sun
Times and Sunday Times

You may also get *almost* daily news from the *Herald Tribune*, printed in Paris and sold each day, except Saturday and Sunday, in all of England

THESAURUS OF ENGLISH TO AMERICAN WORDS

> Americans do speak differently than Brits. Why?
> "The Americans are identical to the British
> in all respects except, of course, language."
> —Oscar Wilde
> "We (the British and Americans) are two countries
> separated by a common language."
> —G. B. Shaw

A
ACCIDENT TOUT	Ambulance chaser
AESTHETIC	Beauty or taste, often pretentious
AFTERS	Dessert
AGONY AUNT	Dear Abby, etc. (advice columns)
AGREE VERDICT	Consent decree
AIT	Islet
A-LEVELS	Similar to SATs; necessary for college entrance
ALIGHT	Get off
ALL MY EYE	Baloney
ALL OVER THE SHOP	Mess, unkempt, out of place
ALLOWANCE	Exemption
ALMONER	Social worker
ALMS HOUSE	For the poor, destitute people with no home
ALUMINIUM	Same as aluminum
ANORAK	Hooded, waterproof jacket with warmth
ANOTHER PLACE	House of Lords (from House of Commons)
ANSAFONE	Answering machine
ANTI-CLOCKWISE	Counterclockwise
APARTMENT	One-room; fat; bed-sitter
APPRISE	Inform
APPROVED SCHOOL	Detention or reform school

ARRIVAL HALL	Reception for guests: castle, manor house, palace
ARSY-VARSY	Vice versa
ARTERIAL ROAD	Main road, major road, trunk road
ARTICULATED LORRY	Truck trailer or buses connected by cab to semi hitch
ASSESSOR	Adjuster
ASSISTING THE POLICE	Held for further questioning
ASSIZES	Court sessions
ASSURANCE	Insurance
AT CLOSE OF PLAY	"When all is said and done"
AT THE END OF THE DAY	Ultimately; finally
AT THE CRUNCH	Churchill: "When the chips are down"
AUBERGINE	Eggplant
AU PAIR	Providing room and board
AUTOCUE	Teleprompter for speakers or TV
AVERSE	Unwilling

B

BABY-WATCHER	Babysitter
BACKHANDER	Graft and corruption
BACKSPANG	Take advantage by trick or legal twist
BAD HAT	Bad egg; naughty
BAD SHOW!	Worst of luck; no good
BAGMAN	Traveling salesman
BAIRN	Baby (Northern England and Scotland)
BAKEHOUSE	Bakery
BALDERDASH	Nonsense
BANDAGE	Elastic bandage strip
BANDY-LEGGED	Bowlegged
BANGERS	Sausages
BANGERS AND MASH	Sausage and mashed potatoes
BANG OFF	Right now!
BANG ON	Right on the nose
(THE) BANK	Bank of England
BANK HOLIDAY	Legal holiday

BAP	Roll or bun for hamburger
BARGAIN	Stock market transaction
BARGE-POLE	"Won't touch with a ten-foot pole!"
BARMAN	Bartender
BARONET	Member of the lowest hereditary knighthood; Bart
BARRISTER	Trial lawyer
BARROW	Pushcart; prehistoric grave or burial mound
BASE RATE	Prime rate
BASH ON	Get on with it
BATHING COSTUME	Swimsuit/bathing suit
BATHING DRAWERS	Briefs, swim trunks
BATON (TRUNCHEON)	Billy club, nightstick
BATSMAN (CRICKET)	Batter
BATTERY RAZOR	Rechargeable shaver
BE UP STANDING (COURT)	Rise as judge, magistrates enter court
BEANS AND BACON	Pork and beans
BEAR IT IN MIND	Think about it
BEASTLY	Unpleasant; unbearable
BED AND BREAKFAST/B&B	Overnight accommodation
BED-BOARD	Headboard
BEDDING	Single annual plant
BED-SITTER	One-room apartment
BEEFEATER	Yeoman Warder Guard of Tower of London; gin
BEER AND SKITTLES	Ninepins game titled Bed of Roses
BELL	Giving a *bell* is giving a *ring* (telephone)
BELLIBONE	A fair maiden, rather beautiful and good
BERM	Shoulder of the road, edge, verge
BESOT	Intoxicate; befuddle; infatuate
BESPOKE	Made to order; custom made
BETHEL	Chapel
BICKIE	Cracker or biscuit
BIG FOUR (Banks)	National Westminster, Barclays, Lloyds, Midland
BIKE	Motorbike (motorcycle)

BILL	Check; policeman
BIN	Hopsack: bread, orderly, waste, litter, dust,
BIRO	Ballpoint pen
BISCUIT	Cookie, cracker, sweet biscuit
BITS AND BOBS	Odds and ends
BIT THICK	Bit much; going too far
BITTER	Strong beer with high alcohol conten
BLACK PUDDING	Blink sausage: suet, pork, and pig's blood
BLACK SPOT	Danger for accident or trouble; often black ice
BLATHER	Talk nonsense, witter, waffle
BLEEZED	Start feeling one's liquor
BLIGHTER	Pain, low character, pest, nag
BLIMEY!	Holy mackerel; expression of surprise; contempt
BLIND ROAD	Dead-end street, cul-de-sac
BLINKING	Euphemistic: bloody
BLOKE	Chap, pal, guy
BLOODY	Awful oath, lousy, bleeding, blinking, bally, ruddy
BLOW LAMP	Blowtorch
BLOWER	Telephone
BLUE STILTON	World-class blue-veined cheese
BLUESTOCKING	Lady devoted to real literature
BOATER	Straw hat
BOBBY	Cop, P. C., peeler, bogey
BODGE UP	Dream up something
BODKIN	Large hatpin; tape needle
BOILED SWEETS	Hard candy
BOILER SUIT	Coveralls
BOKO	Nose (beak)
BOLLICK	Bawl out
BONK	Having sex
BONNET	Hood of car or woman's hat tied under chin
BONNIE	Rather lovely (Scotland)
BOOB	Goof, jail

BOOK	Make reservation for food, lodging, travel
BOOKING FIRM	Brokerage house
BOOKSTALL	Newsstand
BOOT	Trunk of car
BOTTOM	Foot of; far end; stiff upper lip
BOUNDER	Low-bred and cantankerous
BOWLER	Hat from Derby, Billycock, pitcher, (cricket), bocce
BOWLS	Outdoor bowling game on greens
BOX	TV (telly)
BOXING DAY	First day after Christmas, prezzies to servants,
BRACE	Libation; stiff drink
BRACE ME UP	Help
BRACES	Suspenders and some garters
BRACKEN	Large ferns
BRANDY-BUTTER	Hard sauce
BRASS PLATE	Shingle
BRASSED OFF	Pissed off, teed off
BRASSERIE	Type of restaurant, often beef
BRAZIER	Special heater
BRAZING LAMP	Blowtorch
BREAD ROLL	Bun
BREAKDOWN VAN/TRUCK	Tow truck, carrier
BREECHES	Knee-length trousers
BREW UP	Make tea
BRIGADIER	Officer rank between colonel and major general
BRILL	Terrific
BRILLIANT	Great, terrific, awesome
BRIMSTONE	Sulfur, except in sermons
BRITISH BUILDING SOCIETY	Savings and loan
BROAD BEAN	Lima bean
(THE) BROADS	Low-lying wetlands in Norfolk
BROLLY	Umbrella
BTA	Brilliant Travel Answers

BUBBLE AND SQUEAK	Mashed potato mixed with veggies in a fried patty
BUBBLY	Champagne
BUCKET DOWN	"Rain cats and dogs"
BUCKS FIZZ	Mimosa (alcoholic drink)
BUFFER	Bumper
BUFFET	Snack bar
BUGGER	Scamp, scoundrel, pest (a bit vulgar)
BUGGER OFF	Get lost!
BUILDING SOCIETY	Savings and loan bank
BUM	Hinder; rear end, derriere
BUMF	Toilet paper; waste paper; trash
BUNGALOW	One-story house
BUNKER	Refuel
BUNKERED	Out of sorts; fouled up
BUREAU	Secretary
BUSKER	Street entertainer
BUTTERED EGGS	Scrambled eggs
BUTTONS	Bellhop
BUZZ OFF	Cheese off, scram, get lost
BYE	A run in cricket

C

CABOOSE	Galley on shipboard
CAB-RANK	Taxi stand
CACHE	Hiding place
CACHET	Distinction or prestige
CAFÉ	Coffee shop
CALENDAR	Catalog
CALL DIVERSION	Call forwarding
CALL-BOX	Telephone booth, kiosk, telephone box
CALOR GAS	Propane
CANDYFLOW/CANDY FLOSS	Cotton candy
CANNABIS	Marijuana
CANNON	Carom (in billiards)
CANOODLE	Cuddle amorously

CANTEEN OF CUTLERY	Silver set
CANTERBURY	Magazine rack
CANVAS	Tarp; tent; material for painting
CAPSICUM	Green pepper
CARAVAN	House trailer
CAR BREAKER	Wrecker; tow truck
CAR PARK	Parking lots with fees; caravan parks also
CARRIAGE	Car, coach, hansom cab, rail car; one's stature
CARRIAGE RUG	Lap robe, throw
CARRIAGEWAY	Divided highway
CARRY ON	Speak at large, often to a bore
CASKET	Jewelry box; burial coffin
CASUALTY	Emergency
CAT'S EYES	Rubberized reflectors in street; gleam for safety
CATAPULT	Slingshot
CAT BURGLAR	Second-story man (thief)
CAVEAT	A warning: "Beware!"
CENSER	Smudge pot for burning incense
CENSOR	Critic or guard who excises the inappropriate
CENTRE STRIP	Median divider/wall
CENTURY	One hundred runs in cricket
CERTIFIED	Bonkers, loony, insane
CHAMBERMAID	Hotel maid
CHAMBERS	Lawyer's office
CHAMPERS	Champagne
CHANCE-CHILD	Illegitimate love child
CHANCELLOR	Honorary university head; head of House of Lords
CHANCELLOR OF EXCHEQUER	Secretary of the Treasury
CHAP	Guy, fellow, lad
CHAPPIE TATIES	Mashed potatoes (Scotland)
CHAR	Cleaning woman
CHARABANC	Excursion bus
CHARLIE	Nerd, idiot, jerk
CHARTERED ACCOUNTANT	CPA

CHARTERED SURVEYOR	Licensed architect
CHATTING HER UP	Coming on to a girl or woman
CHEEKY	Rude, sassy, pert
CHEERIO!	Bye-bye, ta-ta, so long, see you later
CHEERS!	Skol! Prosit! A Votre Sante! Chin-chin! (a toast)
CHEESED OFF	Teed off, brassed off; get lost
CHELSEA	Affected, often genuine, often Bohemian
CHEMIST	Pharmacist
CHEQUE	Check
CHESTERFIELD	Sofa; often a man's topcoat
CHICORY	Endive
CHIEF BRIDESMAID	Maid of honor
CHIEF EDITOR	Editor in chief
CHIMNEYPIECE	Mantelpiece
CHIN-CHIN	Greeting or farewell; a toast
CHIN WAG	Chatter, talk, gossip
CHIP IN	Butt in, interfere, break in; contribute to
CHIPPINGS	Gravel or small stones
CHIPS	French fried potatoes
CHIT	Memo, often as IOU; cheeky young girl
CHRISTIAN NAME	First name, given name(s)
CHRISTMAS PUDDING	Plum pudding
CHUFFED	Delighted or disgruntled
CHUNNEL	Channel tunnel linking the UK and France
CHUNTER	Natter on and on
CINEMA	Movie house
CIRCULAR ROAD	Belt highway
CIRCUS	Open space; intersection with converging streets
THE CITY	The square mile of inner London
CLEARWAY	No-parking thoroughfare
CLENCH	Rigid
CLERK OF THE WORKS	Supply or maintenance man
CLEVER DICK	Wiseacre
CLOAKROOM	Washroom, restroom

CLOSE	Dead-end residential area
CLOSE THE DOORS, PLEASE	"All aboard"
CLOTTED CREAM	Thick Devonshire cream
CLOUD CASTLE	Continuous daydreaming
COACH	Intercity bus
COARSE	Common
COCKEREL COCK,	Young rooster
COCKNEY (London)	Accent, characteristics of East Enders
COCK-UP	Real mess, total muddle
COD	Joke, parody, tease, spoof; trial balloon
CODSWALLOP	Baloney, nonsense, horse around
COFFEE-STALL	Street coffee stand
COLLECTED	Picked up, retrieved
COLLIER	Coal freighter; coal miner
COLLINS	Roofer
COMB-OUT	Thorough search
COME A CROPPER	Failure in almost anything; have a bad fall
COME-BY-CHANCE	Love child
COME DOWN	Graduate
COME TOP	Win
COMEBACK	Oomph!
COMMERCIAL TRAVELLER	Traveling salesman
COMMISSIONAIRE	Doorman, usually pensioned military men
COMMISSIONER OF OATHS	Notary public
COMMODE	Chamber pot holder
COMMON	Land held in public common; village green
COMMONER	Anyone below the rank of peer
COMMONS	House of Commons: lower legislative chamber
COMPERE	Master of ceremonies, emcee
COMPULSORY PURCHASE	Condemnation and forcible sale
CONCESSION	Discount at movies (not popcorn, pop, etc.)
CONFECTIONER'S	Candy store
CONJUROR	Magician
CONK	Beak, nose; noodle (head)

CONSERVANCY	River or port commission
CONSERVATOIRE	Music school
CONSTABLE	Policeman below rank of sergeant
CONSTITUENCY	District
CONSULTANT	Specialist: cardiologist, pediatrician, gynecologist
CONTINENTAL QUILT	Duvet
CONTRACT HIRE	Lease
COOKER	Stove
COOMB	Valley on side of short hill
COPPER	Policeman
COPPERPLATE PRINTING	Engraving
COR ANGLAIS	English horn; sometimes tenor oboe
CORDS	Corduroy
CORN	Dough; dough (as in money)
CORNET	Ice cream cone
CORRIDOR	Aisles in rails
CORRIE	Scottish mountainside hollow
COSTERMONGER	Fruit and vegetables vendor with pushcart
COSTUME	Lady's bathing or business suit
COUNTERFOIL	Stub, especially for checkbook
COUNCIL HOUSE	House built by local authority and rent subsidized
COURGETTE	Zucchini
CRACKER	Snapper (festive occasions); biscuits; noisy,
CRACKERS	Loony, nuts, loco
CRACKING	Full of pep
CRASH BARRIER	Guardrail
CRAVAT	Ascot tie
CREAM CRACKER	Unsalted, white cracker
CREAMED POTATOES	Mashed potatoes
CREAM TEA	Afternoon tea (4:00 p.m.) with Devonshire cream
CRECHE	Day nursery
CREDIT SLIP	Deposit slip
CREDULOUS	A bit naive, gullible, able to believe anything

CRICKET	Britain's national sport; fairness; deep honor
CRISPS	Potato chips
CROCODILE	Line of children followed by teachers or leaders
CHEQUE	Bank draft or check
CRECHE	Day nursery; Christian scene at Christmas
CRUMPET	Nut (head); dish (desirable female); light muffin
CRUTCH	Crotch
CUBBY	Glove compartment
CURATE	Priest holding spiritual charge, a parish
CURRENT ACCOUNT	Checking account
CUT	Tipsy
CUTE	Shrewd
CUTLERY	Flatware or silverware
CUT UP	Cut off: Upset, overwrought, disturbed
D	
DAFT	Crazy or stupid
DAILY WOMAN	Cleaning woman
DAINTY	Finicky, picky, hard to please
DAME	Conferred knighthood for a lady
DAMMEREL	Effeminate man
DAMPERS	Flat cakes
DASHED	Damned
DAVENPORT	Writing table, escroitoire
DEAD ON	On the nose, "spot on"
DEAN	Head of a cathedral
DEAR	Expensive or costly; term of endearment
DEATH DUTIES	Estate tax
DEFUSE	Remove the dangerous item or moment
DEGREE DAY	Commencement day
DEMERARA	Raw cane sugar, often light brown, for coffee
DEMISTER	Defroster
DENTISCALP	Toothpick or other form of tooth scraper
DESSERT	Fruit course at end of meal; sweets

DEVIL ON HORSEBACK	Prune wrapped in bacon
DEVONSHIRE CREAM	Clotted cream(scalding milk skimmed, rise to top)
DIY	Do-it-yourself choices with stores to help
DIARY	Appointment book
DICEY	Touch and go
DIDDLER	Cheater or swindler
DIGESTIVE BISCUITS	Rather like graham crackers with flavored topping
DIGS	Room to rent, lodging
DINKY	Cute or cunning
DIPPED HEADLAMPS	Lowered bright lights of a car
DIRECTLY	As soon as
DIRECTOR	Executive, even chairman or manager
DIRECTORY ENQUIRIES	Information from phone attendant
DISHY	Most attractive, often sexy
DISPATCH	Mailing and handling
DISPENSER	Vending machine; pharmicist, chemist
DIVERSION	Detour; diverted traffic
DOCTOR'S SURGERY	Doctor's office
DODGY	Cunning; artful; questionable
DOLE	Unemployment benefits
DOLLOP	Serve or cover in large quantities
DON	College teacher; head; fellow
DONKEY'S YEARS	A long, long time
DOSH	Money/cash
DOTTY	Feeble-minded, silly, absurd
DOUBLE-BEDDED	Room with a double bed (queen- or king-size)
DOUBLE CREAM	Heavy whipping cream
DOUBLE-GLAZED	Special, multiglass storm windows
DOWN TRAIN	Train *from* London
DOWNS	Uplands
DOYEN	Dean
DRAPER'S SHOP	Haberdashery, dry goods
DRAUGHTS	Checkers; beer from tap

DRAWING ROOM	Living room
DROP-HEAD	Convertible
DUAL CARRIAGEWAY	Divided highway; boulevard with center median
DUD CHEQUE	NSF; rubber check
DUMBWAITER	Lazy Susan; built-in conveyor to upper rooms
DUSTBIN	Garbage can
DUTCH	Wife (Cockney)
DUVET	Eiderdown quilt
DV, WP	God willing; weather permitting

E

E. C. G.	EKG
EFFECTS NOT CLEARED	Uncollected funds, assets
ELASTOPLAST	Band-Aid
ELECTRIC FIRE	Electric heater
ELEGY	Sorrow, lament, honor to the dead
ELEVATOR	Lift
ELEVEN	Cricket or soccer team
EMPLOYMENT SECRETARY	Secretary of labor
EN SUITE	Hotel or B&B room with bathroom (loo)
ENDIVE	Chicory
ENDORSE	Record an offense on a driving license
ENGAGED	Telephone line engaged; "busy signal"
ESQ.	Esquire: gentleman by birth, man of distinction
ESTATE AGENT	Realtor or broker
ESTATE CAR	Station wagon, SUV, large family car
EVER SO	Very (e.g., beautiful, thoughtful, etc.)
EXCEPT FOR ACCESS	No through trucks or large equipment
EXCHEQUER	Treasury department
EX-DIRECTORY NUMBER	Unlisted
EXPORT CARRIAGE	Overseas shipping
EXPRESS	Special delivery

F
FAG	Toil; exhausting; drag; cigar/cigarette; gay
FAGGOT	Crone or old slut; homosexual
FAGGOTS	Spiced meatballs
FAIRY CAKE	Cupcake
LORRY	Truck
FALL OUT WITH	Have a bad disagreement
FALL OVER BACKWARDS	Bend over backwards; amenable; helpful
FANCY ONE'S CHANCES	Have high hopes
FARE STAGE	Bus fare zone limit
FARRIER	Blacksmith
FASCIA (FACIA)	Dashboard; store board or sign
FAT RASCAL	Soft bun filled with black currants
FELICITATE	Congratulate
FELLOW	Member of college governing body
FENDER	Bumper
FETE	Fair or gala events
FILLET	(fillay) Tenderloin
FILTER SIGN	Green arrow on traffic signal for turn
FIRE	Heater; let go in business
FIRE BRIGADE	Fire department
FIRE-GUARD	Fire screen in fireplace (ingle)
FIRE-RAISING	Arson
FIREPLACE	Ingle
FIRST FLOOR	Second floor
FIRTH	River estuary; narrow arm of the sea
FISH 'N' CHIPS	Fish fried in batter with chips (french fries)
FISHMONGER'S	Fish store
FITTER	Plumber; mechanic
FIVER	Five British pound note
FIXTURE	Scheduled sporting event
FIZZY DRINK	Pop, soda
FLAG DAY	Tag Day—solicit and give to numerous fine causes
FLAKE	Chocolate stick in ice cream
FLAMING	Bloody, "damned," flipping, ruddy

FLANNEL	Face cloth
FLAT	Apartment; dead battery; flat tire
FLAT OUT	At top speed
FLEET STREET	Center of the press, papers, media (formerly)
FLEX	Electric cord, extension
FLICKS	Movies
FLIPPING	Similar to bloody but more polite
FLOAT	Petty cash fund
FLUTTER	Gamble
FLY-OVER	Overpass (usually for pedestrians)
FOLLY	Whimsical structure intended to tease, deceive
FOOTBALL	Soccer
FOOTWAY, PAVEMENT	Sidewalk
FOREBEAR	Those before us, ancestors
FORECOURT	Front yard
FOREIGN OFFICE	State department
FORTNIGHT	Two weeks
FOURBALL (golf)	Foursome
FOUR HONOURS (bridge)	Any four of top five cards in trump suit
FOUR STAR (gas, petrol)	Premium fuel
FREE HOUSE	A pub not affiliated with a brewery
FREEFONE	Toll-free number
FREEHOLD	Title (in real estate)
FRENCH BEANS	String beans
FRESH BUTTER	Sweet butter
FRIENDLY SOCIETY	Mutual insurance group
FRIGHTFULLY	Awfully, very
FRILLIES	Undies
FRINGE	Bangs
FROCK	Dress
FRONT	Seaside promenade
FRONT BENCH	Cabinet ministers; opposite: is "Shadow Cabinet"
FROSTED FOOD	Frozen food
FRUIT MACHINE	Slot machines

FRUITERER	Fruit vendor
FULL MONTY	Mooning, baring one's behind; last bit
FULLY FOUND	All expenses paid
FUNERAL FURNISHER	Undertaker
FUNKY	Chicken, cowardly
FURZE	Plant with sharp thick spines and yellow flowers

G

GAFFER	Old duffer; manager or boor
GALLOP	Bridle trail
GAMMON	Ham; humbug; deception
GAMMY	Lame
GAMP	Bumbershoot: large brollie; golf-size umbrella
GANGWAY	Aisle
GARIBALDI	Currant cookies
GATEAU	Rich layer cake
GAWDELPUS	"God-help-us," exasperating person; real pain!
GAZUMP	Jack up (such as price after agreed sale)
GEARING	Leverage
GENERAL POST	Circulation
GEORDIE	Native of Tyneside; dialect that is hard to follow
GEORGE	Drone pilot, automatic or remote plane pilot
GET ONE'S COLOURS	Make the team
GET ONE'S SKATES ON	Get going
GET ON SOMEONE'S WICK	Get on some nerves, bugging one
GET STUCK IN	Restart an old task
GET THE CHOP	Bumped off; murdered; be fired
GET THE STICK	Catch hell; severely criticized
GET THE WIND UP	Be scared or nervous, even jumpy
GET WEAVING	Get going
(DON'T) GET YOUR KNICKERS IN A TWIST	Not a big thing out of a small thing

GEYSER	Home water heater
GIDDY FIT	Dizzy spell
GIDDY-GO-ROUND	Merry-go-round, carousel
GILT	Object covered with gold
GILTS	Government bonds
GIN AND FRENCH	Martini (also gin and Italian)
GIN PALACE	Pub, bar, saloon
GINGER	Homosexual
GINGER-UP	Pep talk
GIPPY TUMMY	Diarrhea
GIRL GUIDE	Girl Scout
GIVE (TO ONE IN CHARGE)	Turn over to police
GIVE ONE SOME STICK	Give 'em hell!
GIVE THE GATE	Show them the door
GIVE WAY	Yield
GLASS FIBRE	Fiberglass
GLASSHOUSE	Greenhouse; stockade; lock-up
GLASSPAPER	Sandpaper
GLASWEGIAN	One from Glasgow, Scotland
GMT	Greenwich Mean Time (basis for the world)
GO (BRIDGE)	Bid
GOAT	Fool
GOB	Trap; mouth
GOBSMACKED	Stunned, pleased, excited, unexpected
GOBSTOPPER	Like an all-day sucker
GODS (THEATRE)	Peanut heaven, peanut gallery
GO FOR SIX	Get smashed
GO OFF	Bored, tired of someone or something
GO OFF THE BOIL	Slowly simmer down
GO TO THE COUNTRY	General elections for MP (Commons) that occurs every five years
GO UP	Enter college/university; promotion at work or club
GOGGLE-BOX	TV, boob tube, idiot box
GOLDEN HANDSHAKE	Fired (retired) with bonus; golden parachute
GOLDEN SYRUP	Corn syrup

GONE OFF	Spoiled, gone bad
GONGS (MILITARY SLANG)	Hardware such as medals/miniature decoration
GOOD SHOW!	Nice work
GOOD VALUE	Neat stuff
GOOD WALLOW	Strong self-pity
GORSE	Furze (prickly evergreen shrub: yellow flowers)
GOULASH (BRIDGE)	Deal next hand sans shuffling; Hungarian "hash"
GOVERNOR	Warden; boss; *guv'nor* (from cab driver, barman)
GPO	General post office; Royal Mail
GRAMOPHONE	Phonograph
GRANARY BREAD	Delicious dark bread with roughage removed
GRASP THE NETTLE	Take the bull by the horns; "bite the bullet"
GRASS	Rat on, squeal; informer, stool pigeon
GREASE-PROOF PAPER	Waxed paper
GREASY	Slippery: roads, playing courts, devious people
GREAT HALL	Very large hall for entertaining vast audiences
GREAT WAR	World War I
GREEN CARD	Insurance card covering motorists from abroad
GREEN GROCER'S	Selling only fruit and/or vegetables
GRETNA GREEN	Dumfriesshire, Scotland Quick weddings for most
GRID (NATIONAL)	Map reference system helps a find place quickly
GRILLS	Steaks and chops
GRIP	Narrow ditch; bobby pin
GRIT	Fine gravel
GROTTY	Cruddy, ropy, tatty, cheesy
GROUND	Cricket; pitch for soccer (football)
GROUND FLOOR	First floor

GROUND-NUT	Peanut
GUARD	Conductor; brakeman; in bridge, stopper
GUILDHALL	Town hall, city hall
GUILLOTINE	Cloture; act of closing debate in parliament
GUINEA	British pound plus ten to twenty cents (archaic)
GUMBOOTS	Rubber boots
"GUV"	Pal, crony, buddy, chap
GUY FAWKES DAY	Named for perpetrator of failed Gunpowder Plot
GYMKANA	Horse show, even sports car meet (not German)
GYM VEST	T-shirt

H

HABERDASHERY	Notions store (In the States: men's clothing, etc.)
HAGGIS	Dish: minced lamb, entrails of sheep, boiled in sheep's stomach in heavy gravy (Scotland)
HAIR GRIP/HAIR-SLIDE	Hairpin or bobby pin
HALF	Half past, as in "half past twelve"; half pint of beer
HALF CROWN	Half a British pound (archaic)
HALF TESTER	Semi-four-poster bed
HALF-AND-HALF	Mix of ale and stout (or mild and bitter)
HALF-DAY	Day when shop(s) close at 1:00 p.m. or as stated
HALL	Large public room
HARD CHEESE	Tough luck!
HARE OFF	Scat, get out of here
HAULAGE CONTRACTOR	Trucking/moving company
HAVE A BASH AT	Give it a go
HAVE A DOSS	Get some shut-eye (sleep)
HAVE A WORD WITH	Speak to (often important)
HAVE IT OFF	Bring it off; win a bet; make it
HAVE JAM ON IT (JAMMY)	Have it easy

HAVE SOMEONE ON	Kid someone; get him going
HAVE SOMEONE ON TOAST	Hold someone at your mercy
HAVE SQUARE EYES	Be a TV addict
HAVE THE PENNY AND THE BUN	Have your cake and eat it too!
HAVE SOMEONE UP	Bring charges against someone or sue them
HEAD	Principal/dean/ school headmaster; top of bottle
HEADED PAPER	Letterhead
HEADLAMP	Headlight
HEATH	Natural, wild land with shrubs, trees, and plants
HEDGEROW	Stone wall, some made up of hedges
HEEL BAR	Shoe repair shop while you wait
HER MAJESTY'S STATIONERY OFFICE	Government printing office
HGV (HEAVY GOODS VEHICLE)	Semitrailer or eighteen-wheel trailer
HIDEY-HOLE	Hideaway
HIGH STREET	Main street or thoroughfare in towns/villages
HIGH TEA	Light supper (6:00 p.m): may include eggs sausages, cocoa, bacon, Bovril, kippers, jams
HIRE-AND-DRIVE	Rental car
HIRE-PURCHASE	Installment plan
HIRE-PURCHASE-SNATCHBACK	Repossession
HIVE OFF	Split off from main group
HOARDING	Billboard
(NO) HOARDING	Post no bill
HOIST	Freight elevator
HOLD WRONG END OF STICK	Miss the point
HOLDALL	Carryall
HOLIDAY	Vacation
HOME RUN (RACING)	Home stretch
HOMELY	Homey, not fancy or pretentious, unassuming
HOMEY	A homebody, one who loves one's home
HOOD	Convertible top

HOO-HA	Uproar, set-to
HOOP (CROQUET)	Wicket (also in cricket)
HOOTER	Big nose; car horn; plant whistle
HOOVER	Vacuum cleaner; to clean rugs, etc.
HOSEPIPE	Garden hose
HOSTELRY	Inn
HOUSE FULL	SRO (standing room only)
HOUSEMAID	Chambermaid
HOUSEMAN	Intern
HOUSEWIFE	Sewing kit
HOUSING ESTATE	Residential development
HOW ARE YOU KEEPING?	How have you been?
HOWLER	Boner
HUMANE SOCIETY	Lifesaving service
HUMBLE PIE	Eat crow
HUNTER	Pocket watch with hinged covers
HURDLER	Jumping horse; steeplechase
HYPER-MARKET	Mall

I
i	Information; maps, directions, etc.
I SAY	Say! Or, you don't say!
ICE	Ice cream; ices of various flavors
ICE LOLLY	Flavored ice on a stick
ICING SUGAR	Powdered sugar; king sugar
I'LL BE GLAD IF YOU WILL	Please
I'M EASY (ABOUT IT)	It's all the same to me
IMPERIAL	Terrific
IN A FLAP	Het up, bothered
IN A FLAT SPIN	Rattled (flying, headed for likely crash!)
IN HAND	Still time left; under control; not to worry
IN (SOMEONE'S) BAD BOOKS	"In dutch" with someone
IN THE HUNT	In the running
IN TRAIN	Coming along; all in good order; best of form
INDEX	Auto registration
INDUSTRIAL ACTION	Union protest, even to a strike
INGLE-NOOK	Chimney corner

INLAND	Domestic (Inland Revenue is same as IRS)
INTERIOR SPRUNG	Innerspring mattress
INTERNAL	Domestic
INTERVAL	Intermission (play, concert, event)
INVALID'S CHAIR	Wheelchair; mobility
INVERTED COMMAS	Quotation marks
IRONMONGERY	Hardware store
IT ISN'T TRUE	How incredible!
IT'S YOUR GO	It's your turn
IZZARD	Letter Z; can also be *zed* or *zebra*

J

JAB	Injection; shot
JACK	Handyman, odd-job chap
JACKET POTATO	Baked potato
JAM	A real treat
JAUNTY	Master-at-arms; head policeman on a ship
JAW-JAW	Unending conversation
JELLY	Gelatin; Jell-O
JEREMIAH	Gloomy Gus
JERRY	Chamber pot (potty)
JERSEY	Pullover; sweater; jumper
JIGGERED	Worn out, pooped; up the creek
JIGGERY-POKERY	Hanky-panky
JOE BLOGGS	John Doe; Joe Doakes
JOHNNY	Guy
JOINER	Carpenter
JOINT	Roast (beef, lamb, or pork)
JOLLY (good)	Mighty decent of you
JUG	Pitcher
JUGGERNAUT	Big truck (lorry in England)
JUMBLE SALE	Rummage sale
JUMP THE QUEUE	Get ahead of someone in line
JUMPER	Pullover (woman's, generally)
JUST A TICK	Just a moment; right with you

K

KBB	King's Bad Bargain: undesirable serviceman
KEEN ON	Elevates enthusiasm
KEENEST PRICES	Best buys, bargains
KEEP A STRAIGHT BAT	Fair play (from cricket)
KEEP (ANIMALS)	Raising or breeding
KEEPER	Museum/rail guard; custodian in asylum, zoo
KENDAL GREEN	Green woolen cloth
KERBS	Curbs at edge of streets, even in country
KERFUFFLE	In a dither, much ado, fuss, commotion
KIBBLE	Mine bucket; kibbled wheat is cracked wheat
KING'S (QUEEN'S) EVIDENCE	State's evidence
KIP	Rooming house and room; take a nap
KIPPER	Smoked herring; kid or tot is a nipper
KIRBY GRIP	Bobby pin, hair-slide, hair grip
KISS OF LIFE	Mouth-to-mouth resuscitation, CPR
KNACKERED	Worn out, beleaguered
KNAVE	A jack in playing cards
KNICKERBOCKERS	Knickers, trousers often worn in golf
KNICKERS	Men's briefs, perhaps from knickerbockers
KNIFE-AND-FORK TEA	High tea with meat or fish; light supper
KNOCK	Wow (impress), as in "knock 'em dead"
KNOCK ME UP	Wake by phone or door knock; get pregnant
KNOCK ON	Turn up; arrive
KNOCKER	Door-to-door salesman
KNOCK-OUT	Volleying; exhausting; eliminate others
KO	Kickoff (British football); knockout (boxing)

L

LABOUR EXCHANGE	State employment office
LACQUER	Hair spray
LAND AGENT	Realtor
LAND OF THE LEAL	Loyal (Scotland); for most, heaven

LANDED	OK for some things; little luck; land of gentry
LANDLORD	Innkeeper or pub keeper
LANDSLIP	Landslide
LARGE	Double portions
LARK	Job; type of activity
LASH OUT	Throw money around
LAST POST	Taps
LAVATORY ROLL	Toilet tissue
LAY	Set (the table); a special tax laid on citizens
LAY (ONE) BY THE HEELS	Track (someone) down
LAY-BY	Rest stop by edge of road (no facilities)
LEA/LAY	Pasture
LEAD FOR THE CROWN	Act as chief prosecuting attorney
LEADER	Editorial; chief counsel; concertmaster
LEATHER	Chamois
LEAVING GIFT parachute	Retirement prezzies; maybe a golden
LECTURER	Instructor
LEFT LUGGAGE OFFICE	Baggage room; sometimes, lost luggage
LEGO	Building blocks for children; started in Eton
LET	Rent or lease a house or apartment
LET-OUT	Loophole
LETTER POST	First-class mail
LETTER-BOX	Mailbox, postbox
LICENCED	Own a liquor licence (hotels, pubs, restaurants)
LIE DOGGO	Lie low (play dead, like some dogs do)
LIE DOWN UNDER	Buckle under
LIE IN	Sleep late
LIFE VEST	Life jacket
LIFT	Elevator
LIGHT COME, LIGHT GO	Easy come, easy go
LIMEY	American GI's name for Brits during wars
LIMITED COMPANY	Corporation, as in incorporated
LINERS	Underpants (worn under knickers)

LINK HOUSE	Row of joined houses; terrace
LINKMAN	Anchorman; moderator; go-between
LINO	Linoleum
LISTENING ROOM	Control room
LIVER SAUSAGE	Liverwurst (goose liver)
LIVERISH	Bad temper
LIVERPUDLIAN	From/of Liverpool
LIVERY	Costume
LIVING (ECCLESIASTICAL)	Curate, vicar, rector, etc.
LOAN SHARE, STOCK	Bond
LOCAL	Neighborhood bar
LOCH, LOUGH	Lake or inlet (Scotland/Ireland)
LOLLY	Dough (money)
LOLLYPOP MAN (WOMAN)	School traffic guide
LOMBARD STREET	London's money market
LOO (WC)	Toilet, restroom, washroom, water closet
LOOK SMART!	Get a move on
LOOK-OUT	Outlook
LOOK-OUT WINDOW	Picture window; oriel; look-through window
LOOSE CHIPPINGS	Loose gravel
LOOSE COVERS	Slipcovers
LOOSE WATERPROOF	Slicker
LORD CHAMBERLAIN	Head of management of the royal household
LORD CHANCELLOR	Chief justice (presides over the House of Lords)
LORRY	Truck; articulated lorry: trailer truck; some vans
LOST PROPERTY OFFICE	Lost and found
LOUD-HAILER	Bullhorn
LOUGH	Lake or stream
LOUNGE	Living room (smaller than great hall)
LOUNGE SUIT	Business suit
LOVELY!	Great! Fine! Wonderful! Marvelous! Terrific!
LOYAL OPPOSITION	Party not in power
LUCERN (LUCERNE)	Alfalfa

LUCKY-DIP	Grab bag
LUD	Lord (pronounced "lud" when addressing a judge)
LUMBER	Junk; clutter
LUMBERED WITH	Saddled with (see also *landed with*)
LUMBER-ROOM	Storage room
LUNCHEON VOUCHER	Lunch coupon

M

MA'AM	Proper form to address the queen
MAC	Short for mackintosh (raincoat)
MACADAM	Blacktop; tarmac; metalled road
MAD ON	Crazy about
MADE REDUNDANT	Dismissed from a job, usually with pay
MAGISTRATE	Justice of the peace
MAÎTRE D'	Head waiter
MAKE	Bring or fetch
MAKE A DEAD-SET AT	Make a play for
MAKE GAME OF	Make fun of
MAKE OFF WITH	Run through (money, assets); squander
MAKE OLD BONES	Live to a ripe old age
MAKE THE RUNNING	Take the lead
MAKE UP	As in, fill the prescriptions
MAN	Once, valet; now, my good man; man I live with
MAN OF THE MATCH	Most valuable player
MANAGER	Producer
MANAGING DIRECTOR	Executive vice president
MANOR	Domain, bailiwick; beat (police)
MARCHING PAPERS	Walking papers
MARGE	Oleomargarine
MARK	Covering an opposing player
MARKET GARDEN	Truck farm
MARKS & SPARKS (store)	Marks & Spencer: clothing, furnishings, food, etc.
MARQUEE	Large tent or awning for celebrations
MARQUESS	In Britain, just below duke

MARQUIS	Familiar form of address for marquess
MARRIAGE LINES	Marriage certificate
MARROW	Squash (oversized zucchini)
MARTINI	In pub it means vermouth; ask for gin and French
MASH	Mashed potatoes; "chappie taters" (Scotland)
MASHED NEAPS	Mashed turnips (Scotland)
MASTER OR MISTRESS	Teacher
MATCH	Game
MATCHCARD	Scorecard
MATE	Buddy
MAZE	Bewilder
MEAD	Honey-laced liquor
MEAT-SAFE	Food cupboard
MENTIONED IN DISPATCHES	Cited for bravery, heroism
MERCHANT BANK	Investment bank
METALLED ROAD	Paved road; metal plates in road
(THE) MET(S)	London police
METRE	Actual units for measuring
MEWS	Lodgings (once, cages and stables)
MI5	Military intelligence, counter-intelligence and key Protection against terrorism and other threats
MICKEY	One acts satirically or teasing
MIDDLE NAME	Nickname
MINCE	Chopped meat
MINCEMEAT TART	Mince pie
MIND	Watch out for; care; mind the step
MINDER	Bodyguard
MINERAL	Soft drink, soda
MINI	Morris Minor (car from the '50s); skirts
MINICABS	Freelance cabs hired only by phone
MINISTER	Cabinet member
MINSTER	Cathedral
MISFIELD	Error, as in sports
MIZZLE	Drizzle

MOBILE POLICE	Police cars
MOBILE PRODUCTION	Traveling show
MOLE	Little hill; outer breakwater near harbor; spy within
MONEY-SPINNING	Fund-raising; spinning draws big money
MONGER	Dealer (such as fishmonger)
MONKEY-FREEZING	Fiercely cold
MONKEY-NUT	Peanut
MONOMARK	Approved, registered ID card
MOONLIGHT FLIT	On the lam; flight to avoid capture or even charges
MOONRAKER	Blockhead
MOONSHINE	Castles in the sky, visions, wild dreams
MOOR	Open wastelands; heather-bound
MOT	Motor; place for required annual car inspection
MOT CERTIFICATE	Decal vehicle inspection certificate (required}
MOTHERING SUNDAY	Mother's Day (fourth Sunday of Lent)
MOTOR	Drive
MOTOR COACH	Intercity bus
MOTOR HORSE BOX	Horse van
MOTOR-BIKE	Motorcycle (bike)
MOTORCAR	Automobile, car
MOTORWAY	Freeway; divided highway
MOVING STAIRWAY	Escalator
MP	Member of parliament (Commons)
MUCKER	Take a spill; wild expenses; buddy or pal
MUDGUARD	Fender; wheel arch; wing
MUFFIN	Light, flat, often spongy cake; crazy fool
MULL	Mess up
MULTIPLE SHOPS	Chain stores
MULTI-STOREY	High-rise buildings
MUSIC-HALL	Vaudeville theater
MUTES	Hired pallbearers
MY SHOUT	My round (of drinks)

N

NAFF	Tacky; unfashionable
NAIL VARNISH	Nail polish
NAN	Granny; grandma
NAPPY	Diaper
NARK	Rat; stool pigeon; annoy
NARKED	Aching
NARKY	Bitchy; untamed
NATIONAL HEALTH SERVICE	Medical insurance through government
NATTER	Chatter
NAUGHT	Nothing
NAUGHTY	Wicked; rude
NEAR-SIDE LANE (TRAFFIC)	Slow lane
NEEDLE MATCH	Grudge match
NERVY	Jumpy
NETS	Sheers that go between curtains and windows
NEWMARKET (HORSES)	Horse-racing town; card game; tight-fitting coat
NEWSAGENT	Dealer in papers, magazines, etc.
NEWSREADER	Newscaster
NEWS-ROOM	Magazines, papers, periodicals in library
NEXT DOOR BUT ONE	Two doors away
NICE BIT OF WORK	Almost anything qualifies; quite a "dish"
(THE) NICK	Station house; in good shape (pink of condition)
NICK/NICKED	Steal something; be arrested
NICKER	GB pound; quid
NIL	Nothing; also in scoring (e.g., 24 to nil (O)
NIPPER	Little child
NIPPY	Make it snappy! Also, a waitress
NOBBY	Wealthy, elegant, smart, distinctive
NOMINY	A tale, a tall story
NOSE TO TAIL	Bumper to bumper
NOSEY-PARKER	Nosy, even a gossiper
NOSH	Food

NOT HALF	Not half bad; all good
NOT ON YOUR NELLY	No way
NOTECASE	Billfold
NOTICE BOARD	Bulletin board
NOUGHTS AND CROSSES	Tic-tac-toe
NUDE CONTRACT	Void contract
NUMBER PLATE	Auto licence plate

O

OAP	Old age pensioner; senior citizen
OAST	Kiln for drying HOPS
OAT CAKE	Round biscuit: eaten circa 3 December
OATS	Oatmeal, porridge
OBLIQUE	Slash, stroke
OCTINGENTENARY	Eight hundredth anniversary
ODDMENTS	Odds and ends
OFF CUT	Remnant
OFF LICENSE	A shop may sell liquor all day for use off premises
OFF ONE'S OWN BAT	In cricket, on one's own
OFFER for SUBSCRIPTION	Public issue invitation
OFFICIAL	Officer
OFF-SIDE LANE	Passing lane on motorway or dual carriageway
OFF-THE-PEG	Ready-to-wear (off-the-rack)
(THE) OLD BILL	Cops
OLD LADY OF THREADNEEDLE STREET	The Bank of England
OLD PARTY	Old-timer
OLD SCHOOL TIE	Old boy
OLD SOLDIER	Old hand
OLD SWEAT	Old soldier
OMNIUM GATHERUM	Collection(s) of persons or things; a part for all
ON THE CHEAP	Less expensively
ON THE DAY	When the time comes
ON THE LOOSE	On a spree

ON THE RIGHT LINES	On the right track
ON THE SLATE	In pubs: on the tab, on the cuff, on tick
ON THORNS	On tenterhooks
ONE-OFF	One-time occurrence
ORDINARY CALL (PHONE)	Station-to-station
ORDINARY SHARES	Common stock
ORGANIZE	Round up
(THE) OTHER HALF	Another drink
OUTGOINGS	Expenses
OUTSIZE	Extra large (XL)
OVEN-GLOVE	Pot holder
OVER THE MOON	Moments of sheer rapture
OVER THE ODDS	Above market value
OVER THE TOP	Going too far, too much
OVERLEAF	On reverse side
OVER-REACH	Hold on to a stock or bond too long
OVERTAKE	Pass on the road

P
PACK	Deck of cards
PACK IT IN	Leave, depart; retire; quit
PACK UP	Quit; conk out
PADDY	Tantrum; short temper
PAGETT, M. P.	Whirlwind tourist; "he knows all" even in short visit
PALETTE-KNIFE	Spatula
PANACHE	Elan; flair; swagger
PANDA CAR	Police car
PANTECHNICON	Moving van
PANTS	Underpants (Brits call pants "trousers")
PARADE	Promenade; shopping, line of shops; bands
PARAFFIN	Kerosene (American paraffin is white wax)
PARISH	Smaller local town; local Church of England
PARK	Car park (town parking); caravan park
PARKING BAY	Space for vehicle

PASS	In school exams: O-level pass; A-Level pass; honours
PASSAGE	Corridor
PASTY	Knish, pie, tart
PATIENCE	Solitaire card game
PAVEMENT	Sidewalk
PAY FOR THE CALL	Accept reversed charges
PAY ON THE NAIL	Pay only in cash
PAY ONE'S SHOT	Chip in; ante; share
PAY-BOX	Box office
PAYING DESK	Sales counter; cash register
PAYING-IN SLIP	Deposit slip
PC	Privy councillor; police constable; politically correct
PEARLY	Fruit and vegetable pushcart vendor; costermonger
PECKISH	Empty; a bit hungry
PEEP-TOES	Open-toed shoes
PEG AWAY	Keep on keeping on
PEG OUT	Kick the bucket; pack it in; pop one's clogs
PELICAN CROSSING	Pedestrian, light-controlled street crossing
PENCE	Penny
PENSIONER	Retired senior citizen
PERAMBULATOR	Baby carriage
PERGOLA	Trellis
PETROL	Gasoline
PG	Paying guest; boarder
PICCADILLY	A kind of stiff collar; Eton collar; famous pub
PILLAR-BOX	Mailbox
PINCH	Swipe or steal; arrest; nab
PINNY	Apron
PINT	Beer or bitters
PINTA	Pint of milk
PIP	Pay telephone that beeps to alert user to deposit more coins; call is recorded

PIP	Blackball; wound; pull rank; at post (win by a nose)
PIT	Rear of orchestra; front is stalls
PLAICE	A flat fish, on many menus
PLAIN	Homely
PLASTER	Band-Aid
PLAY A STRAIGHT BAT	Fair play
PLAY-PIT	Children's sandbox
PLIMSOLLS	Sneakers
PLONK	Cheap wine
PLOUGHMAN'S LUNCH	Bread, cheese, butter, onions, jar of beer perhaps
PLUM DUFF	Plum pudding
PLUS FOURS	Golfing knickers
PNEUMATIC	Car tire (archaic)
PNEUMATIC DRILL	Jackhammer
POINT	Socket for electric cords, appliances
POINTSMAN	Copper (police); railroad switchman
POLO NECK	Turtleneck; roll neck; collars turned down
PONTOON	Blackjack
POP	Hock or pawn
POP OFF	Leave
POP YOUR CLOGS	"He died with his boots on"
POPLIN	Broadcloth
POPPER	Snap; stud
POPSIE	Cutie
PORRIDGE	Oatmeal (cooked); also, to be in the clink for a while
PORTER	Doorman; sometimes, a hall porter
PORTMANTEAU	Small carrying bag
POST	Mail (Royal Mail)
POST RESTANTE	General delivery
POSTAL COURSE	Correspondence or online course
POSTAL SHOPPING	Mail-order shopping
POSTAL VOTE	Absentee ballot
POST-BOX	Mailbox
POST-CODE	Zip code

POST-FREE	Postpaid
POULTERER	Poultry merchant
PRAM	Baby carriage
PRANG	Crash land (aircraft); bomb (target); bump
PRAT	Oaf, idiot, ne'er-do-well
PRAWNS	Large shrimp
PRECIPITOUS	Edge of danger; rashly may embarrass
PREFECT	Monitor (helps keep order and prevent cheating)
PREFERENCE SHARES	Preferred stock
PREMIUM BOND	Government lottery bond
PRENTICE	Inexperienced hand
PRESENTER	Newscaster
PRESS-UP	Push-up
PREZZY	Gift or present
PRICEY	Dear; expensive
PRIVATE SCHOOL	Prep school (public school)
PROCTOR	College monitor (for matters of discipline); program
(THE) PROMS	Series of late summer concerts in Royal Albert Hall
PROPELLING PENCIL	Mechanical pencil
PUB	Public house (similar to saloon and tavern)
PUB GRUB	Finger food served in some pubs
PUB THEATRE	Drama, music, poetry performed in pubs
PUB-CRAWL	Make the rounds of various pubs
PUBLIC PROSECUTOR	District attorney
PUBLIC SCHOOL	Private school (similar to prep school)
PUBLICAN	Pubkeeper, landlord
PUB-TIME	Times for opening/closing pubs
PUDDING	Dessert (also "afters" or "sweets")
PUDDING CLUB	Being pregnant
PUKKA	Genuine, but not overwhelming or "smashing"; of Hindu origin
PUNCTURE	Flat (tire)
PUNKA(H)	Ceiling fan

PUNTER	Bettor or speculator; one guiding boat (punt) on water
PURCHASE TAX	Excise tax (now known as VAT, value-added tax)
PURSE	Not handbag; known as "money pouch"
PUSH	Be fired; get the gate
PUSH BIKE	Bicycle; two-wheeler; bike is motorcycle
PUSH OFF	Go away! Scat! Scram!
PUSH THE BOAT OUT	Do more than expected; your turn to pay
PUSH-CHAIR	Stroller
PUSHED (FOR)	Pressed (for) time, answer, goods, etc.
PUSH-PIN	Thumbtack
PUT A FOOT WRONG	Screw up, err
PUT A SOCK IN IT	Stow it! Stop!
PUT BY	Procrastinate
PUT DOWN	Put to sleep; charge to my account; fold one's hand
PUT (ONE) IN THE PICTURE	Bring one up to the moment
PUT IT ACROSS (SOMEONE)	Punish; let 'em have it!
PUT (SOMEONE) OFF	Disturb; spoil the moment; disappoint
PUT ONE'S SHIRT ON	Bet your last dollar
PUT THE KETTLE ON	Make tea for one and all
PUT THE SHUTTERS UP	Fold in a card game; declare insolvency
PUT-U-UP	Hide-a-bed; convertible couch

Q
QUARTER LIGHT	A vehicle's vent window
THE QUEEN	Stay to end of dance; loyal toast to the Queen
QUERY	A complaint; uncertain of exact location
QUEUE	"Cue"; line of people:
QUID	One British Pound
QUITE	For sure! or up to snuff

R
RAC	Royal Automobile Club
RAF	Royal Air Force

RAG	Tease; stunts; gags; hard stone
RAG-AND-BONE MAN	Waste or junk man
RAKE UP	Bring back bad memories or moments
RAMP	Speed bump or a racket, such as a swindle
RANDY	Horny
RATE	Local tax
RATHER	And how!
RATTY	Out of sorts
RAVER	Stunning; gorgeous beauty
RAZZLE	Go on a spree or binge
REACH-ME-DOWN	Ready-made
READ	British universities (to major in)
READER	Associate professor or lecturer
READING GLASS	Magnifying glass
RECORDED DELIVERY	Certified mail
RECOVERY VAN	Tow car or wrecker
RED BIDDY	Cheap red wine, plonk
RED RAG	Red flag (warning or alert)
REDIRECT	Forward mail
REDUNDANT	Fired or made unemployed by layoff
REEL	Spool
REFER TO DRAWER	Insufficient funds (NSF: not sufficient funds)
REFUSE TIP	Garbage dump or waste
REGISTER OFFICE	Marriage clerk's office
REGISTRY	Employment agency for maids, servants
REMEMBRANCE SUNDAY	Sunday nearest 11 November to honor all vets
REMOULD	Retread tires (tyres)
REMOVALS	Moving
REPAIRING LEASE	Tenant: pays maintenance, taxes; net to lessor
RESTAURANT CAR	Dining car (now known as buffet car)
RESURRECTION PIE	Dish of leftovers
RETURN	Round-trip ticket on air, bus, liner, etc.
RETURN POST	Undeliverable mail

(THE) REVENUE	Inland Revenue Service; Internal Revenue (IRS)
RIDE	Forest path for horseback riding
RIGHTO!	Sure! OK! (also, rightio, right ho, carry on)
RIG-OUT	Attire or outfit
RING	Ring up, *not* call up
RING ROAD; RINGWAY	Beltway or bypass (circular road around town)
RIPPING	Great (as in "ripping" good time)
RISE	Raise in salary; gain in investment(s)
RISING POWDER	Baking powder
ROAD	Way
ROAD UP	Highway sign indicating road under repair
ROAD WORKS	Sign indicating men working
ROAD-SWEEPER	Street cleaner
ROOF-RACK	Vehicle luggage rack
ROUGH WORK	Heavy work (around the house); tough guy
ROUND	Sandwich; round of ham/beef; route
ROUND THE BEND	Crazy
ROUNDABOUT	Traffic circle; intersection moving clockwise
ROVER TICKET	Unlimited travel ticket, or park, or events
ROW	Quarrel
ROYAL	Member of the royal family
RUBY	Agate (type size)
RUCK	Common herd; also-rans; rugby scrum
RUDDY	Bloody, damned
RUDE	Inconsiderate; frank; indecent; rude (robust) health
RUMBLE STRIP	Speed bump
RUM-BUTTER	Hard sauce; brandy butter for pies, puddings, apples
RUMP STEAK	Sirloin
RUN IN	Break in new auto
RUNNER BEANS	String beans
RUNNING ACCOUNT	Checking account

RUSTICATE	Expel from school (temporary); sent down (permanent)
S	
SACK	Dismissal, fire, expel
ST. MICHAEL	Patron saint of hangover-prone sailors
ST. VITUS DANCE	Vigorous, writhing moves of the body
ST. WILGEFORTE	Protector from troublesome husbands
SALAD	Chicken, beef, ham and lettuce, some veggies
SALOON	Car type; hair-dressing, beauty, billiards (not parlor)
SALT BEEF	Corned beef
SALT CELLAR	Salt shaker
SARNIE	Sandwich
SAUCE	Cheeky; rude
SAUCE-BOAT	Gravy boat
SAVE ONE'S BACON	Save one's skin (life)
SAVINGS CERTIFICATES	CDs
SAVOURY	A flavor: not sweet; salty, herbal, or sour; tidbit
SCAB OFF	Take off; get lost
SCHOOL-LEAVER	High school graduate
SCHOONER	Large sherry or port glass
SCOFF	Good eats; wolf, gobble, or scarf down food
SCONE	Baking powder biscuit, often with tea
SCORE OFF	Winning arguments or rebuttals
SCOTLAND YARD	Highest UK law enforcement agency (like FBI)
SCREE	Mountain slope; pebbles, rocks coming down hill
SCREW	Wages and profit; old run-down horse; raw item for a bin
SCREWED	Tightly closed; loaded
SCRIBBLING-BLOCK	Scratch pad
SCRIMSHANK	Goldbrick, slacker, shirker

SCRUFFY	Messy
SCRUMP	Hard cider from apples on ground
SCRUMPULATE	Rob orchards of fruit
SCULLERY	Back kitchen
SEA FRET	Fog
SEE (SOMEONE) OFF	Reprimand, chastise, discipline
SEE THE BACK OF	See no more
SELL	Letdown; often, buyer's remorse
SELL (SOMEONE) A DUMMY	Put it over on someone (rugby term)
SELL (SOMEONE) A PUP	Stick it to someone; cheat; mislead
SELL UP	Sell out
SELLOTAPE	Scotch tape
SEMI-DETACHED	One family house joined to another by a wall
SEMI-SKIMMED MILK	2 percent milk
SEMOLINA	Cream of Wheat
SEND DOWN	Expel or rusticate
SEND TO COVENTRY	Ignore; avoid; turn one's back
SENIOR SERVICE	Royal Navy
SERGEANT-MAJOR	Top sergeant; sometimes, topkick
SERVERY	Service counter or checkout counter
SERVICE FLAT	Hotel apartment (residential hotel)
SERVICE LIFT	Dumbwaiter
SERVIETTE	Napkin
SET ABOUT	Lay into
SET DOWN	Drop off (bus, taxi, train)
SET LUNCH	Table d'hôte; prix fixe (preset meal and price)
SET TEA	Afternoon tea (traditionally around 4:00 p.m.)
SHAKE DOWN	Hospitality by giving a bed for the night
SHANDY	Mix of beer and lemonade
SHARED LINE	Multiline phone service
SHEAF	Wad of paper money; bankroll
SHEMOZZLE	Mix-up; boondoggle
SHEPHERD'S PIE	Minced roast with mashed potatoes

SHILLING	Approximately fourteen US cents (based on current exchange rate)
SHIRE	County
SHOE MENDER	Shoemaker; cobbler
SHOOT	Hunt; shooting party; shooting practice; shooting area
SHOOT THE MOON	Slip out of town at night; moonlight flit
SHOPPING TROLLEY	Shopping cart
SHOP-WALKER	Floorwalker
SHORT	Drink (unmixed)
SHORT BACK AND SIDES	Crew cut; very short cut
SHORT TIME	Part-time or even a temporary worker
SHOUT	My turn to buy food, drinks, etc.
SHOW A LEG	Get up and go!
SHOW ONE'S COLORS	Stand up and be counted
SHOW-HOUSE	Model home, apartment, or condo
SIDEBOARDS	Sideburns
SIDESMAN	Deputy churchwarden (junior warden)
SIGN OFF	Initials as confirmation
SILVER STREAK	English Channel
SILVERSIDE	Top round (steaks, etc.)
SIMPLE	"not all there"
SINGLET	Men's undershirt; T-shirt
SINK DIFFERENCES	Get over it, bury the hatchet
SIRLOIN	Porterhouse (steak); rump steak is Sir Loin (knighted by king in humour)
SISTER	Head nurse in a hospital; Church of England nun
SIT AN EXAM	Take an exam
SITE	Locale
SITTER-IN	Babysitter
SITTING-ROOM	Living room
SITUATIONS VACANT	Help wanted
SKINT	Broke
SKIP	For large trash (dumpster); college servant
SKIPPER	Captain in cricket

SKIRTING	Baseboard
SKIVE	Goldbrick; scrimshank; swing it
SKULK	Hide; stay away; shirk
SLAG	Criticize
SLAP-DOWN	100 percent in favor
SLAP-UP	Bang up job!
SLATE	Pan, criticize; be merciless
SLEDGE	Sled
SLEEPAWAY	Die of natural causes
SLEEPING PARTNER	Silent partner (in business)
SLEEPING POLICEMAN	Speed bumps
SLEIGHT	From skill and ability to sly and cunning
SLIP ROAD	Access road
SLOANE RANGERS	Wealthy, well-dressed, well-connected ladies
SLOOM	To sleep heavily, rather soundly
SLOSH	Smack (hit)
SLOW OFF THE MARK	Not quick on the uptake
SLOW TRAIN	Local (versus express)
SMALL AD	Classified ad
SMARMY	Oily
SMASHING	Terrific; gobsmacking!
SMITHFIELD-BARGAIN	Match or marriage for monies; bought wives
SMOOTH IN	Get settled
SNAPPER	Fastener (dressmaking, tailoring)
SNIG	Small eel
SNIGGLER	One who catches eels
SNITCH/GRASS	Traitor, user, liar
SNOG	Neck, kiss
SNOOKERED	In a tight spot
SNORTER	Humdinger; bloodied nose
SNORTING	Fantastic
SNUFF IT	Pop one's clogs, kick the bucket
SNUGGERY	Place to relax, get away from it all; den
SOD OFF	Get lost
SOD'S LAW	Murphy's Law

SOLDIER ON	Stick with it
SOLICITOR	Lawyer (general practitioner), rarely in trial
SOMMELIER	Head of wines at a restaurant; provides choices for patrons
SORBET	Flavored Ice; served between courses to help clear palate
SORT IT OUT	Work it out; get it done
SOT OFF	Scram, go away
SOUTH BANK	Long string of art venues
SPAGHETTI JUNCTION	Cloverleaf on highways
SPANNER	Wrench
SPARE GROUND	Vacant lot
SPARKING PLUG	Spark plug
SPATE	Flood
SPATULA	Tongue depressor
SPEND A PENNY	Go to the loo; go to toll toilet
SPINNEY	Thicket; small woods
SPIRITS	Hard liquor
SPIV	Sharp operator (just within the law)
SPOIL	Dirt and things from excavated hole
SPONGE BAG	Toilet kit
SPONGE FINGER	Ladyfinger (biscuit)
SPOT	Spot of tea; pimple; decimal point; e-mail "dot"
SPOT ON	Quite right! Perfect! Correct!
SPOTTED DICK	Suet pudding with currants and raisins
SPRING GREENS	Young cabbage
SPRING ONION	Scallion
SPRING ROLL	Egg roll (Chinese)
SQUARE	Paper napkin; mortar board (graduates); all even
STAGGERER	Blow to ego; retort; rebuttal; riposte
STALL	Outdoor stand; orchestra seat (theatre)
STAND	Run for office
STAND DOWN	Quit; retire; withdraw; delay
STAND ONE'S OWN	Hold fast

STANDARD LAMP	Floor lamp
STAR TURN	Headliner in theatre; top-notch performer
STARING	Loud style or colours; talk incoherently
STARKERS	Bare naked
STARTERS	Appetizers
STATE SCHOOL	Public school
STATION-MANAGER	Station agent
STEP OUT	Hurry up!
STICK OUT	Hold fast to one's point of view
STICKY PLASTER	Band-Aid
STICKY TAPE	Adhesive tape
STICKY WICKET	Tight situation in cricket
STING	Soak a man by price, object
STOCKHOLDER	Livestock farmer/breeder
STOCKIST	Retailer
STONE	Weight measurement; equal to fourteen pounds
STONE CLADDING	Stone facing
STONY	Broke
STOOGE ABOUT	Kill time
STOOPGALLANT	Humbles the great; makes some mere men
STOPPAGE	Wage deductions
STORE	Warehouse
STOREY	Various building levels
STOUT	Dark, full-bodied beer
STRAIGHT AWAY	Immediately
STRAIGHTENED OUT	Fixed
STRAITEN	To restrict or limit
STREET	Social class; "up your alley"
STRETCHER	Gurney
STRIKE OFF	Disbar; remove license
STRUCK ON	Crazy about; nuts about; stuck on!
STRUNG UP	High-strung; het up
SUBJECT	Citizen
SUBSCRIPTION LIBRARY	Lending library
SUBWAY	Pedestrian underpass

SULTANA	White raisin
SUMP	Crankcase
SUN-BLIND	Awning
SUN-TRAP	Sunny or a sheltered place
SUPERANNUATION SCHEME	UK pension plan
SUPPORTER	Best man
SUPREMO	Governor; overseer
SURGEON	One who operates; called surgeon, not doctor
SURGERY	GP or dentist's office
SURGICAL SPIRIT	Rubbing alcohol
SURNAME	Last name; given as a birthright
SURVEYOR	Building inspector
SUSPENDERS	Garters (vertical); braces
SUSS OUT	Figure out what is meant or happening
SWACKED	Tight (from heavy drink)
SWEDES	Yellow turnip; rutabagas
SWEET	Really neat! Good. Profitable. Happy moment
SWEETS	Very tasty dessert
SWEET-SHOP	Candy store or counters
SWIMMING COSTUME	Bathing suit
SWISS ROLL	Jelly roll
SWITCHBACK	Scenic railway; roller coaster

T

T JUNCTION	End of road; must turn left or right
TA	Thanks (ta-ta may mean good-bye)
TABLE	Submit (not delay) for discussion
TABLE MONEY	Cover charge
TAFFY	Welshman
TAIL-BACK	Backed up in traffic jams
TAKE AWAY	Takeout (food)
TAKE DOWN	Take a letter; cheat
TAKE FIRST KNOCK	Go first
TAKE IN CHARGE	Detain; arrest
TAKE ON	Catch on

TAKE THE BISCUIT	That takes the cake!
TAKE (MAKE) UP THE RUNNING	Go to the front; set the pace
TALK THE HIND LEG OFF A DONKEY	Endless palaver
TALLY PLAN	Installments
TALLY PLATE	Nameplate
TAP	Faucet
TAPES	Starting lines for race
TAPPED THE CLARET	Got (gave) a bloody nose
TARA	(Pronounced "tah-rah") good-bye
TARADIDDLE	Lie, fib
TARIFF	Schedule of charges
TARMAC	Tarred road; in front of airport terminals, hangars
TART	Pie; rather tawdry woman
TA-TA	Bye-bye
TATER, 'TATUR, TATIE	Spud; potato
TATTY	Grotty; shabby
TAXI RANK	Taxis lined up for fares, but in sequence
TEASE	A really tricky job or problem
TEA-TOWEL	Dish towel
TELEPHONE BOX	Call box; kiosk
TELEPHONIST	Switchboard operator
TELLY	TV
TENNER	Sawbuck; ten-pound (GB) note
TENSION	Knitting gauge
TERMINUS	Terminal
TERRACE	Row of joined houses
TERRACES	Standing room in sports
TEST BED	Proving ground; iron framework to rest items tested
TEST MATCH	International match (similar to World Series) in cricket or rugby
TESTER	Four-poster bed
THAT'S JUST THE JOB	That's the ticket!
THAT'S TORN IT	That does it!
THEATRE	Operating room

THERE'S NO SHIFTING IT	It's unshakable
THIN ON THE GROUND	Few in number
THIRD-PARTY INSURANCE	Liability Insurance
THIRD PROGRAMME	BBC: Radio 3 for intellects, art lovers, high brow
THREEPENCE (THRUPPANCE)	Three pennies (archaic)
THROGMORTON STREET	London: Bank of England; Wall Street (UK style)
THROUGH	Connected; still in contention
THUMPING	Greatly
THUNDER MUG	Chamber pot for bathroom
TICK	Check in marking forms
TICKET TOUT	Scalper
TICKET-OF-LEAVE	Parole
TICKLER	Poser
TICK OVER	Turn over
TIDDL(E)Y	Tipsy
TIFFIN	Lunch
TIGHTS	Pantyhose
TILL	Through, until
TIME!	Closing time! (at a pub)
THE TIMES	London paper: not *London Times* or *Times of London*
TIN	Can
TIN TACK	Carpet tack
TINKLE	Ring up; phone call
TINNY	Small tin mug or tin of ale, beer
TIP	Dump; waste center
TIP-UP SEAT	Folding seat
TIRESOME	Irritating, aggravating (not boring)
TITCHY BIT	Just a drop or bit of anything
TOAD-IN-THE-HOLE	Sausage in a batter or bun
TOBACCONIST'S SHOP	Cigar and tobacco store
TOFFEE	Taffy
TOLLY	Candle

TON	one hundred miles per hour; darts: extremely rare score
TOODLE	Walk or drive to some place
TOP	Beginning of aisle, street, etc., as at the head of
TOP GEAR	High gear
TOP-HOLE, "TOPPER"	Great; first-rate, best, tip-top
(AT THE) TOP OF THE TREE	Highest rank in one's profession
TOP-UP	Fill 'er up! Top it off!
TORCH	Flashlight
TORTUROUS	Something that spoils and causes anguish
TORY	Member of Conservative Party
TO SHOUT	Buy round of drinks for a group or entire pub
TOSSED	Drunk
TOT	Small dram of whatever
TOTE BETTING	Pari-mutuel betting
TOTEM	Order; hierarchy
TO THE WIDE	Dead-drunk or done in utterly
TOUCH	A special sort of "thing"
TOUT	Checks on horses and sells tips for race(s)
TOWER BLOCK	High-rise building
TRACK	Highway lane
TRADE DIRECTORY BOOK	Yellow pages
TRADE(S) UNION	Labor union
TRAFFIC BLOCK	Traffic jam
TRAFFIC ISLAND	Median
TRAFFIC WARDEN	Parking enforcement officer; meter maid
TRAM	Streetcar (tramcar)
TRANSFER	Decal
TRANSFERRED CHARGE CALL	Collect call
TRANSPORT CAFÉ	Truck stop (24-7)
TREACLE	Molasses
TREAT	Terrific; fuss; special moment
TREWS	Tartan trousers
TRICK CYCLIST	Psychiatrist, shrink

TRIFLE	Sponge cake, whipped cream; custard, gelatin, fruit, sherry
TRILBY	Felt hat
TRIPPER	One going to the shore, country, special places
TROLLEY	Pushcart
TROOPING THE COLOURS	Annual House Guards Parade in Whitehall
TROUSER SUIT	Pantsuit
TROUSERS	Pants
TRUCKLE BED	Trundle bed
TRUNCHEON	Billy; nightstick used by police
TRUNK CALL	Long-distance call
TRUNK ENQUIRIES	Long Distance information
TRY	Touchdown (British rugby)
TUBES	Subway (London Tube); signs say *underground*
TUB-FAST	Sweating a hot tub, then abstinence, to cure viruses
TUB-THUMPER	Soapbox orator
TUCK	Gourmet meal, big eats
TUMBLE DRYER	Clothes dryer
TUMBLE TO	Catch on to
TURF	Sod; neck of the woods
TURN AND TURN ABOUT	Alternately
TURN OUT	Clean up a room, etc.
TURN UP	Sleeves, trousers; sports upset
TURN UP ONE'S TOES	Kick the bucket
TURNABOUT	Reversible overcoat
TWEENY	Assistant to cook and chambermaid
TWELFTH MAN	Standby as replacement for injury in cricket
TWERP	Insignificant person, a nobody
TWIG	Gain understanding
TWIN BEDS	Two single beds
TWIST	Swindle
TWISTER	Sharpie
TWIT	Nerd, oaf, jerk
TWITCHER	Bird-watcher

TWO-SEATER	Roadster
TYRE	Rubber wheel, tire (cars and trucks)

U

UNDER OBSERVATION	Patrolled
UNDERDONE	Rare
UNDERGROUND	Subway, The Tube
UNIT TRUST	Unit managing investments for investors
UP A GUM TREE	Up the creek, bunkered, snookered
UP STUMPS	Pull up stakes
UP THE SPOUT	In deep trouble
UPPER CIRCLE	Second balcony

V

V&A	Victoria & Albert Museum
VARIETY	Vaudeville
VARNISH	Nail polish
VAT	Value-added tax (redeem at airport with receipts)
VAULTS	Burial places inside churches
VC	Victoria Cross (UK's highest military decoration)
VENERABLE	Honored title given to chief deacon of England
VENUE	Location, site, place of meeting
VERGE	Grass shoulder on all highways, roadways
VERGER	Custodian(s); leads clergy to chancel and pulpit
VEST	Undershirt; waistcoat
VICAR	Assistant curate
VICE-CHANCELLOR	President of university (chancellor is honorary head)
VILLAGE	Town (no legal or political definition of a village)
VINTAGE CAR	Veteran (historic) car
VOUCHSAFE	Give, send, deign, grant

W
WAFF	A puff or blast of air or wind (Scotland and northern England)
WAGES SHEET	Payroll
WAGGON	Train car
WAITS	Christmas carolers
WALKABOUT	Campaign stroll
WALKING FRAME/ZIMMER	Walker
WALKING-SUPPER	A supper (one dish is passed around for all)
WARDER	Prison guard
WARDOUR STREET	Center of the film industry (like Hollywood)
WARDSHIP	Custody
WASH LEATHER	Chamois
(THE) WASHING UP	Do the dirty dishes
WASHING-UP-BOWL	Dishpan
WASSAIL	Wash one's throat with ale; drinking vessel
WASTE BIN	Wastebasket
WATERSPLASH	Ford a brook or stream
WAY OUT	Exit
WC	Water closet; toilet; loo, bathroom
WEATHER-BOARD	Clapboard
WEB LETTUCE	Iceberg lettuce
WEDGE	Wad of bills (money)
WEIR	Dam to hold back waters
WELL AWAY	Tipsy; in horse racing, off to a good start
WELL BREECHED	Well heeled, rich, wealthy
WELL DONE	Spot on! Nice going!
WELLIBOOTS	(Lord) Wellington rubber boots for gardening, etc.
WEST END	Shopping and bits of London; like Broadway
WHACKED	Done in, pooped
WHARF	Dock
WHEELED CHAIR	Wheelchair, invalid chair
WHEELIE BIN	Outdoor garbage bin on wheels
WHEEZE	Clever scheme (good wheeze: go to early movie)

WHINGE, WINGE	Complain, gripe, just be ugly
WHIP-ROUND	Collection by passing the pan, hat, bucket
WHIPSY	Milk shake
WHISKY	Scotch
WHISTLE OFF	Depart on run
WHIT	Pentecost (Whitsuntide), end of Lent
WHITE FEATHER	Note of cowardice
WHITE WAX	Paraffin
WHITEHALL	Seat of British government
WICKET	Hit to score runs in cricket; "sticky wicke*t*" is a difficult situation
WIDE BOY	Sharpie, on the shady side
WIGGING	Dressing down; scolding
WIMPY	Hamburger (as in an American comic strip)
WINDCHEATER	Windbreaker
WINDOW-GAZING	Window-shopping
WINDSCREEN	Windshield
WINE MERCHANT'S	Liquor store
WINE STEWARD	Wine waiter, sommelier
WING	Fender on a vehicle
WING COMMANDER	Lieutenant colonel
WING MIRROR	Side-view mirror in a vehicle
WINGEING	Complaining; crybaby
WINKER	Turn signal on a vehicle
WINKLE OUT	Pump information from a source
WIPE OFF A SCORE	Settle a score
WITTER	Ramble on; blather
WIZARD	Great success
WOLD	Open, uncultivated, wooded upland, oft for sheep
WONKY	Wobbly
WON'T GO	Can't work it out
WOOD WOOL	Wood, lumber shavings
WOODEN SPOON	Booby prize
WOOLLIES	F. W. Woolworth & Co. (still in the UK!)
WOOLLY	Sweater

WORK TO RULE	Do everything by the book
WORK TO TIME	Clock watch
WORKHOUSE	Home for the poor and wretched
WORKING PARTY	Various committees
WORKS	Factory; plant; machinery
WOULDN'T TOUCH IT WITH A BARGEPOLE	Wouldn't touch it with a ten-foot pole!
WRAC	Women's Royal Army Corp
WRAP IN COTTON, WOOL	Spoil; coddle
WREAK HAVOC	Cause or inflict harm, pain
WRENS	Women's Royal Naval Service
WRITING DOWN	Depreciation

Y

(THE) YARD	Scotland Yard
YEOMAN	Small farmer; guard at Tower of London
YIELD TO REDEMPTION	Yield to maturity
YORKER	Fastball pitching in cricket, just under bat
YORKSHIRE PUDDING	Batter, like popovers, baked in pan; with roast beef

Z

Z(ed) CAR	Police car; panda car; jam sandwich
ZEBRA CROSSING	Pedestrian crossing (roads marked in zebra-like stripes)
ZED	The letter Z
ZIP	Zipper
ZIZZ	Wee nap
ZOWERSWOPPED	Bad natured

WHERE TO GO FOR SPECIAL HELP

US EMBASSY, London (no visitors)
24 Grosvenor Square
London W1
Phone: (44 from USA) (0) 20 7499-9000
For **passport help**: call above number
US Passport and Citizenship Unit
    55-56 Upper Brook Street W1
US LEGATION, Edinburgh, Scotland
3 Regent Terrace
Edinburgh EH7 5BW
Phone: (44) (0) 131 556 8315
after hours: (44) (0) 1224 857097
AMERICAN EXPRESS
    6 Haymarket SW1
    020/7930-4411
    01273 696 933 (lost or stolen cards)
CAMERA REPAIR
SEANDEAN, First Floor
    105-109 Oxford St. W1
    020/739-8418
DENTIST—Dental Emergency Care Service
    Guy's Hospital, St. Thomas St. SE1
    020/7955-2186
DOCTOR—**Medcall**
    2 Harley St. W1
    0800/136-106
    Great Chapel Street Medical Center
    13 Great Chapel St. W1
    020/437-9360
DRUGSTORES/PHARMACIES/CHEMISTS
    Zarfash Pharmacy (24-7)
    233-235 Old Brompton Rd.
    020/7373-2708

Bliss Chemist (9:00 a.m. to midnight)
<u>Boots the Chemist</u> (largest in UK)
EMERGENCIES: Dial 999 for police, fire, ambulance
CHILDLINE: 0800-1111
Children needing help or **who are lost.** Call is <u>FREE.</u>
RAPE CRISIS CENTER
020-7837 1600 (twenty-four hours)
SAMARITANS
0345 909090 (twenty-four hours)
For all emotional problems
LOST PROPERTY
London Transport Lost Property Office
200 Baker St. NW1
020/7486-2496
Taxi Lost Property
15 Penton St. N1
020/7833-0996
Buses: 020/7222-1234
Find depots at end of line
NEWSPAPERS
Guardian, Independent, Telegraph, Times (and others). For news from the United States, see the International (Herald) Tribune.

PASSES AND OTHER DEALS

London White Card
Discount pass for London and fifteen major museums and galleries.
Plus Pass allows unlimited travel on tubes and buses for three to seven consecutive days.
Travel Cards
Good for choice travel for one, three, or seven days on both tubes and buses.
Discount Passes
National Express buses and BritRail 35 percent discount on travel passes in UK for seniors
Oyster Pass

For those staying in London, you can "bank" monies for travel on tubes or buses and use the card without paying until it tells you it is about to run out, at which point you can add as needed.

PASSPORTS
Be *sure* passport is current for at least six more months. Make two copies of photo page and keep one at home and one in extra suitcase.

PETROL (Gasoline {petrol} for Diesel or Cars, SUVs, Lorries)
Imperial gallon equals one and one-fifth American gallons; sold in litres (liters). Unleaded is cheapest and best for most cars.

RESTROOMS (Lavatory, Loo, Toilet, WC)
Found in many stores, even on streets, In parks, and Tube stations. May need to pay for some loos. Use coins 10p to 25p

ROYAL MAIL (Post)
Many branches; some postboxes on streets.

VAT
Like American sales tax on most goods, although not on groceries, children's clothes and shoes, takeaway foods, and unprepared foods. **Be sure to get form from clerk at time of purchase for most items; then turn in forms at VAT desk at airport for immediate refunds.**

REMEMBER:
If you choose to drive in the UK you *must* stay to the left at all times. No passing inside other vehicles. At all pedestrian crossings look to the RIGHT!

VEHICLE EMERGENCIES:
AA—0800 887766
GREEN FLAG—0800 400600
RAC— - 0800 828282
YOU MAY USE A GPS WHEN DRIVING IN THE UK but *NOT* a radar detector. National speed limit is (70) seventy miles per hour. It *is* enforced; some roads have hidden cameras, with warnings.

TIPS ON CALLS TO THE USA
AT&T USA DIRECT   0800-89-0011 + number
MCI Call USA   0800-89-0222 + number
SPRINT EXPRESS   0800-89-0877 + number
PHONE USA   0800-89-0456 + number
OR
Dial 155 for collect/reverse charges calls

RESOURCES AND ACKNOWLEDGMENTS
A <u>Dictionary of Slang</u>
English Slang of the UK
J.M. Duckworth (1996)
www.peevish.co.uk/slang/
Beautiful Britain magazine (2010)
PO Box 52
Cheltenham, Gloucesterhire GL50 1YQ
Website: *beauitfulbritain.net*
Best Houses (England's Thousand)
Simon Jenkins, Quintin Wright (photographer)
Viking Studio (2003)
Penguin Group (USA) Inc.
375 Hudson Street
New York, New York 10014
www.tumblr.com/tagged/England-s-thousandbesthouses
Britain Magazine (2010)
Official magazine of Visit Britain
The Chelsea Magazine Company
26-30 Old Church Street
Chelsea, London SW3 5BY
Email:*info@britian-magazine.com*
British English, A to Zed
Norman W. Schur
Facts on File Publications (1987)
Excellent summary and definitions of older and newer words in British English It helps sort out the king's (queen's) English.
<u>www.scribd.com/doc/38420199British</u> *-English-a-zed-t*
British Heritage magazine
Published bimonthly by
Weider History Group
19300 Promenade Drive
Leesburg, VA 20176-6500
BritishHeritage@weiderhistorygeoup.com
British Phrasebook, first edition

Elizabeth Bartsch-Parker, Stephen Burger, Richard Crowe, Roibeard O'Maolalaigh, and Dominic Watt
Lonely Planet Publications (1999)
Excellent delineation of words by subject, demography, history, usage, and pronunciation of current slang.
www.goodreads.com/book/show/182841.british_phrasebook
Calendar of Unusual Customs and Traditions:
England, Scotland and Wales
Mandy Barrow
Woodlands Junior School
Hunt Road
Tonbridge Kent TN10 4BB UK
Month-by-month listing of festivals, celebrations, special days, things that seem eccentrieven mad—but carried out year after year.
www.*woodlands-junior.kent.sch.uk/customs/curious/calend…*
Castles and Palaces and Stately Homes of Britain and Ireland
Charles Phillips and Richard Wilson
Anness (2007)
"A magnificent visual account of Britain's architectural and historical heritage celebrated in over five hundred beautiful photographs, fine-art paintings, drawings, and more."
The Country Life Book of Castles and Houses in Britain
Peter Furtado, Nathaniel Harris, Hazel Harrison, Paul Pettit
Newnes Books (1986)
Pertinent historical backgrounds, descriptions, and photographs of great buildings of Britain
Divided by a Common Language
Christopher Davies
Mayflower Press (2002)
Fine tips for tourists. Great on practical information, points on differences in meanings, spellings and what to say and not to say. Best of all, it also points out American words compared to British words.
English Monarchs
www.englishmonarchs.co.uk/crown_jewels.htm
26 September 2011
Explore Britain's Villages

Susan Gordon
AA Publishing (1994)
Location map, photos, places, descriptions.
Fodor's '98 Pocket London
Fodor's Travel Publications (1997)
Great for those making a short trip.
Fodor's upCLOSE Great Britain
Fodor's Travel Publications (2000)
Quite helpful in pointing out country charms, city sights, and tons of practical information about where to go, how to get there, and something about choices and costs.
Forgotten English
Jeffrey Kacirk
William Morrow Paperbacks (1999)
Frommer's Portable London
Frommer's (2000)
Great Britain
Dorling Kindersley (DK) (2000)
Superb historical information with many photos, maps, and layouts—even within buildings telling what's displayed therein.
Great Britain
Fodor's Travel Guides (1986)
Quite factual with practical information for most parts of England, Scotland, and Wales.
Her Ladyship's Guide to the Queen's English
Caroline Taggart
National Trust Books (2010)
From the intro: "What distinguishes the well-spoken Englishman or woman is…whether they use language correctly and, crucially, elegantly."
Historic Houses Castles and Gardens (1995)
Deborah Valentine, editor
Reed Information Services (1995)
Annual publication on more than 1,300 estates.
London in My Pocket
British Tourist Authority (2000)
www.visitbritain.com

Clear suggestions on places to visit, accommodations, and things to see and do. Many clear and easily readable maps.
FREE
London in Your Pocket, third edition
Barron's Educational Series (1987)
Restaurants, hotels, museums, theatres, shops, nightlife, landmarks, and great venues.
Mike's English/American Dictionary
Mike Hetherington (1999)
www.effingpot.com/slang.html
The Most Beautiful Villages in England
James Bentley
Thames and Hudson (1999)
Glorious photographs, notable descriptions, all listed by shires (counties).
National Trust Magazine
National Trust (Summer 2011)
Included in membership. May be purchased separately.
People Weekly
The Decade of Diana
Collector's Edition Extra (Fall 1990)
Time Inc. Magazine Company
Realm Magazine
Published bimonthly by
The British Connection Inc.
116 Ram Cat Alley, Ste. 201
Seneca, SC9678-3263
Scotland Magazine
Published monthly by
Paragraph Publishing
St. Faiths House
Mountergate, Norwich, Norfolk NR1 1PY, UK
Shop London, first edition
Tom Masters, Martin Hughes, and Sarah Johnstone
Lonely Planet (2000)
Offered FREE at HSBC (2009)
Full listings of fine stores of all kinds.

THOUGHTS WHILE FLYING HIGH!

Shoppers' London
Columbus Books (1986)
Pocket guide with maps. Best for high level shopping in special areas.
This England Magazine (multiple issues)
PO Box 52
Cheltenham, Gloucestershire GL50 1YQ
Totally London
Eat London (2005)
Yellow Pages (by phone) 118247
Great for all kinds of meals in many venues.
FREE
Travel Guide to British/American English
Norman Moss
Passport Books (1986)
Travelling in London
London Transport
Maps and sightseeing information.
FREE
Wikipedia Encyclopedia
www.wikipedia.com
FREE